Chris Jacques

Technical English

SECOND EDITION

1

Workbook

T0346060

Pearson Education Limited
KAO Two
KAO Park
Hockham Way
Harlow, Essex
CM17 9SR
England
and Associated Companies throughout the world.

pearsonenglish.com

Written by Chris Jacques

First published 2008
This edition published 2022
Fifth impression 2024
ISBN: 978-1-292-42450-7

Set in Source sans pro-Light
Printed and Bound by Neografia, Slovakia

Acknowledgements

Illustrated by Mark Duffin, Peter Harper, HL Studios and Raja G.

Image Credit(s):

123RF: Gilles Paire 42, indigolotos 16, jumbi 8, lunfengzhe 42

Alamy: Alvey & Towers Picture Library 8, Art Directors & TRIP 19,
Cultura Creative RF 48, Cultura RM 48, Dorling Kindersley ltd 16,
Hugh Threlfall 16, PA Images 29, qaphotos.com 42

Cirbic Inc.: Cirbic Inc. 16

Getty: Bo Zaunders 8, Fuse/Corbis 48, morkeman/E+ Cov, 1

NASA: NASA/JPL-Caltech 63

RunningSnail Ltd: RunningSnail Ltd 15

Science Photo Library: TRL LTD 28

Shutterstock: alvant 8, Atitaph_StockPHoTo 48, Celso Diniz 35,
Goran Algard 50, Surasak_Ch 16, Svitlana Hulko 8, Tatiana
Shepeleva 8, Vladi333 40

The Car Photo Library: David Kimber 09

Woods Hole Oceanographic Institution: ©Woods Hole
Oceanographic Institution, C. Judge 58

Cover images: Front: **Getty Image:** morkeman/E+

All other images © Pearson Education

Contents

1 Check-up

1 Basics

1 **Use the words in the box to complete the dialogues.**

what's   where   what   ~~I'm~~   is   are   I'm

1   **A:**   Hi, __I'm__ Kaito.

   B: Hello, my name _____ Pedro.

   A: Nice to meet you.

2   **A:**   Hello. _____ are you from?

   B: I'm from Japan. _____ is your name, please?

   A: I'm Hans. Pleased to meet you.

3   **A:**   Good to meet you, Svetlana. _____ you from Poland?

   B: No, _____ from Russia. _____ your name?

   A: I'm Danielle.

2 **Use the words in the pool to complete the orders.**

1   Stand _____up_____.

2   Write _____.

3   Turn _____.

4   Close _____.

5   Sit _____.

6   Raise _____.

7   Come _____.

right

down

your name

your book

in

~~up~~

your hand

3 **Write the words in the correct columns.**

~~adapter~~   antenna   bolts   cable   chisel   nuts   plug   saw   screwdriver   screws
spanner   washers

Tools	Electricals	Fixings
_____	_____adapter_____	_____
_____	_____	_____
_____	_____	_____
_____	_____	_____

1 🔊 1.1 **Listen and correct the five mistakes on the business card.**

Rossi Air

Alex Grayson
Aerospace Technician
Tel: + 44 (0)1562 802927
Email: alexg14@rossi.com

2 🔊 1.2 **Listen and complete the form.**

Surname:	J_____
First name:	_____
Company:	_____
Email address:	_____

3 **Match items 1–10 with the right words. Then match items 11–20.**

1	gal	a)	amp/ampere		11	+	k)	kilometres per hour
2	€	b)	angle/degree		12	m	l)	kilowatt
3	kg	c)	Celsius		13	kW	m)	litre
4	A	d)	euro		14	V	n)	metre
5	in	e)	foot		15	kph	o)	negative
6	ft	f)	gallon		16	rpm	p)	positive
7	km	g)	gram		17	W	q)	pound
8	°	h)	inch		18	L	r)	revolutions per minute
9	g	i)	kilogram		19	£	s)	volt
10	C	j)	kilometre		20	–	t)	watt

4 🔊 1.3 **Mr Martin is buying a car. Listen and write down the facts about the car.**

1 Kilometres: _120 000_ km

2 Engine temperature: _____° Celsius

3 Petrol tank: _____ litres

4 Engine speed: up to _____ rpm

5 Top speed: _____ kph

6 Price: _____ euros

3 Dates and times

1 **Write the words for these ordinal numbers.**

4th *fourth*   5th _____

12th _____   29th _____

23rd _____   8th _____

7th _____   31st _____

30th _____   6th _____

22nd _____   20th _____

2 **Complete the puzzles.**

1   Fri 31 Jan → 8 Feb
the thirty-first of January is a Friday, so the eighth of February is a Saturday.

2   Wed 29 Mar → 2 Apr
_____

3   Tue 29 May → 3 June
_____

4   Thur 30 July → 4 Aug
_____

5   Mon 28 Sept → 7 Oct
_____

6   Thur 27 Nov → 6 Dec
_____

3 **Use the words in the box to complete the dialogue.**

that's   is   it's   then   what   ~~when's~~   it's

A: *When's* the meeting?

B: _____ on Monday.

A: _____ that Monday the 12th?

B: Yes. _____ right.

A: Do you know _____ time?

B: _____ at 10 o'clock.

A: OK. See you _____. Bye.

B: Bye.

4 **Look at the clocks and complete the sentences.**

1    2    3    4

1   It's _____*five thirty*_____ in the morning.

2   It's _____ afternoon.

3   _____ evening.

4   _____ at night.

4 Word list

NOUNS (car)	NOUNS	VERBS	PHRASAL VERBS
adapter	amp	first	listen
antenna	Celsius	second	lower
bolt	degree	third	pick up
cable	euro	fourth	put down
chisel	foot	fifth	raise
nut	gallon	sixth	read
plug	gram	seventh	say
saw	inch	eighth	sit
screw	kilogram	ninth	stand
screwdriver	kilometre	tenth	start
spanner	kilometres per hour	eleventh	stop
washer	kilowatt	twelfth	write
counter	litre	thirteenth	**ADVERBS**
flight	metre	twentieth	closed
model	pound	thirtieth	down
platform	revolutions per minute	**PHRASES**	in
surname	volt	Excuse me.	left
	watt	Hello.	off
	ADJECTIVES	Good to meet you.	on
	negative	Nice to meet you.	open
	positive	Pleased to meet you.	out
			right
			up

1 **Make up answers to these questions. Use words from column 2 of the Word list.**

1 How heavy is it? _425 grams_   _22 kilograms_ _____

2 How hot is it? _____

3 How long is it? _____

4 How far is it to Dubai? _____

5 How fast is the car travelling? _____

6 How fast is the engine turning? _____

7 How much petrol is in the tank? _____

8 What's the price of the car? _____

9 How do you write 225 V in words? _____

2 Parts (1)

1 Naming

1 Write sentences for the pictures.

Parts	Vehicles
axle deck nose number plate tail ~~wheel~~	boat motorbike mountain bike plane ~~racing car~~ rocket

 1 *That's the wheel of a racing car.*

 2 _____

 3 _____

 4 _____

 5 _____

 6 _____

2 Use the words in the box to correct the sentences.

bolts   ~~nails~~   nuts   screw   ~~screwdriver~~   spanner   staple   washers

1 *That isn't* _____ a hammer. That's *a screwdriver* .

2 *Those aren't* _ screws. Those _ *are nails* _____ .

3 This _____ a chisel. This _____ .

4 _____ washers. These _____ .

5 _____ a nail. This _____ .

6 _____ nuts. These _____ .

7 _____ a staple. That's _____ .

8 _____ nuts. Those _____ .

2 Assembling

1 How do you change a car wheel? You need:

a **jack**, to raise and lower the car

a **box spanner**, for the nuts

a **spare wheel**

Complete the instructions for the pictures, using the verbs from the box. Some words are used more than once.

loosen	lower	put on	~~raise~~	take off	tighten

1 _____*Raise*_____ the car with the jack.

2 _____ all the nuts with the box spanner.

3 _____ all the nuts.

4 _____ the wheel _____ the axle.

5 _____ the spare wheel _____ the axle.

6 _____ all the nuts.

7 _____ all the nuts with the box spanner.

8 _____ the car.

2 Write the dialogue lines in the right order.

30 mil. How many nails do you need?
30 mil, please.
~~Hello.~~
I need 80, please.
Some nails. What size do you need?
Hello. I need some nails, please.

Shopkeeper: _____*Hello.*_____

Customer: _____

Shopkeeper: _____

Customer: _____

Shopkeeper: _____

Customer: _____

3 Ordering

1 🔊 2.1 **Listen to the two phone messages. Correct the mistakes in the names and numbers.**

1 Name: Vladislaw Sczetin	Phone number: 00 48 920 4516
2 Name: Abdel Mohamed Mabruk	Phone number: 00 20 537 1490

2 🔊 2.2 **Listen to the two phone messages. Complete the message forms.**

1

Date: _____

Time: _____

Caller: _____

Phone number: _____

2

Date: _____

Time: _____

Caller: _____

Phone number: _____

3 🔊 2.3 **Listen to the dialogue. A customer is ordering skateboard parts on the phone. Complete the order form.**

Skateboarders							
ORDER							
Surname: _____							
Address: _____							
_____							
Postcode: _____							
Tel: _____							
Item (circle)	Colour (circle)			Size (circle)			Quantity (write)
Helmet	red	yellow	blue	large	medium	small	_____
Deck	red	yellow	blue	large	medium	small	_____
Pad	red	yellow	blue	large	medium	small	_____

4 Word list

NOUNS	NOUNS	VERBS	ADJECTIVES
axle	bolt	assemble	large
deck	bricks	loosen	medium
helmet	hammer	pull	small
nose	lever	push	red
pad	nail	put	yellow
plate	nut	take	blue
tail	screw	tighten	
truck	screwdriver		
wheel	spanner		
	staple		
	washer		

1 There are eight words in the Word list with double letters. Write them here.
wheel, _____

_____

2 Write the words in column 2 on the correct line.
Tools: *hammer,* _____
Other things: *bolt,* _____

3 Complete the instructions for skateboarding with words from the box. Some
words are used more than once.

loosen   push   ~~put~~   take   tighten

Before skateboarding
___*Put*___ on the helmet.
_____ it down onto your head.
_____ the helmet strap.
_____ on the pads.
_____ the pads.

After skateboarding
_____ the pads and _____ them off.
_____ the helmet strap and _____ off the helmet.

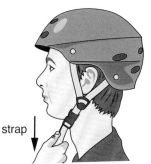

strap

Review Unit A

1 Complete the dialogues.

> I'm   he's   that's   is   do   I'm   ~~are~~

1   *A:* _Are_ you Maria?

   B: No, _____ Sonia. _____ Maria.

2   *A:* What _____ you do, Toni?

   B: _____ a builder.

3   *A:* _____ Carlos a builder?

   B: No, _____ an electrician.

2 Check the information in Course Book page 9. How do people in different countries write dates? Write the dates in column 2.

A person writes . . .		What is the date?
1 Claire	Paris, 1/2/21	*1 February 2021*
2 Vicky	Chicago, 3/9/21	_____
3 Yuki	Tokyo, 21/01/22	_____
4 Matt	Seattle, 11/12/21	_____
5 Director, ISO	Geneva, 2021-07-08	_____
6 Peter	Berlin, 9/10/21	_____

3 Work out the sequence of days and dates 1–3 and keep the same number of days between 4 and 8. Write the missing ones.

1   Monday, the first of May

2   Thursday, the fourth of May

3   Sunday, the seventh of May

4   _____

5   Saturday, the _____ of May

6   _____

7   Friday, the _____ of May

8   _____

1 **Put the letters in the correct order and write the plural words.**

1 lotsb   _bolts_   5 ilsan   _n_____
2 hessraw   _w_____   6 lesax   _a_____
3 wressc   _s_____   7 eatsksarbod _s_____
4 tuns   _n_____

2 **Write another dialogue like the example. Use the words from the box.**

A: What's this tool called?

B: It's a *spanner*.

A: Is it for *nails*?

B: No. It's for *nuts*.

hammer   screws   nails

1 **A:** What's this tool called?

   B: It's _____

   A: Is _____

   B: _____

3 **Complete the dialogue with the questions.**

What's your phone number?	What's your email address?
What's your name?	What size cards do you need?
How many do you need?	What's your address and postal code?
When do you want them?	

A: Hello. I need to order some business cards.

B: _How many_ _____

A: 200, please.

B: _____

A: 85 millimetres by 55 millimetres.

B: _____

A: Stevens, with a V. Initials HC.

B: _____

A: 14 Hayfield Road, Bristol BR7 4JK.

B: _____

A: 0117 893462.

B: _____

A: It's harry.stevens@ojs.com.

B: _____

A: On Friday, please.

3 Parts (2)

1 Tools

1 Complete the crossword. Find the vertical word in the puzzle.

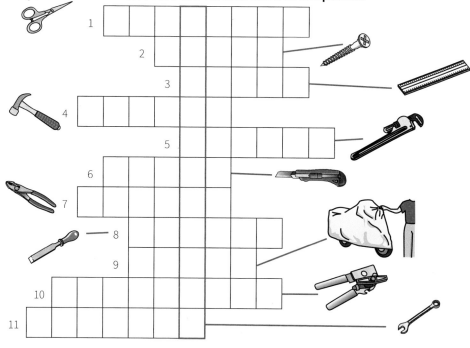

2 Write the answers to the puzzles. Use each item once.

hammer	pair of pliers	pair of scissors	saw	~~screwdriver~~	spanner

1   It has a handle, a shaft and a head. It turns screws. It is a ___*screwdriver*___.
2   It has a shaft and a head. It drives in nails. It is a _____.
3   It has two handles and two blades. It cuts paper. It is a _____.
4   It has a shaft and jaws, but no blades. It tightens nuts. It is a _____
5   It has two handles, jaws and blades. It cuts wire. It is a _____.
6   It has a handle and a blade. It cuts wood. It is a _____.

3 Use the words in the box to complete the dialogues. Some words are used more than once.

do	does	don't	doesn't	have	has

1   **A:** _Does_ Carlos need a spanner?
    B: No, he _____.
    A: _____ he need a pair of pliers?
    B: Yes, he _____.
    A: Does he _____ a saw?
    B: Yes, he _____ two.

2   **A:** _____ you have a hammer?
    B: No, I _____.
    A: _____ you need a hammer?
    B: Yes, I _____.
    A: I don't _____ one. Go and ask Pedro.
        He _____ one in his tool box.

1a Match the word halves.

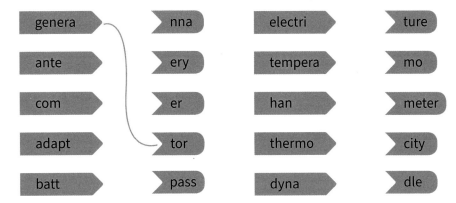

genera — nna — electri — ture

ante — ery — tempera — mo

com — er — han — meter

adapt — tor — thermo — city

batt — pass — dyna — dle

1b Write the full words next to the explanations.

1   This makes electricity. _____*generator*_____

2   This shows North. _____

3   This stores electricity. _____

4   An AC _____ changes AC to DC.

5   This receives radio signals. _____

6   A solar panel changes sunlight into _____ .

7   You can measure the _____ in Fahrenheit or Celsius.

8   You turn this round with your hand. _____

9   This measures temperature. _____

10 This turns and makes electricity. _____

2   Use the verbs from the box to complete the text.

charge   shine   charges   ~~turn~~   listen   turns   produces

Are you going on holiday? This 3-in-1 torch, radio and battery charger is for you.

When you (1) ___*turn*___ the handle, it
(2) _____ the dynamo. This
(3) _____ the battery. You can then
(4) _____ your torch, or
(5) _____ to the radio.

You can also turn (crank) the handle to (6) _____ your mobile phone or laptop.

1 🔊3.1 Listen to the dialogue in the factory. Where does the driver put the boxes? Write the number of the product (1–9) on the correct shelf. Then write all the product names on the correct shelves.

1	speakers	4	scanners	7	mouse pads
2	keyboards	5	headphones	8	adapters
3	flash drives	6	amplifiers	9	printers

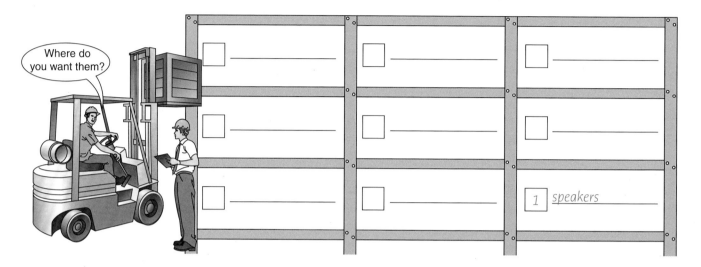

Where do you want them?

1 _speakers_

2 🔊3.2 Listen to a dialogue on a boat. Where do the people put the things? Write the number of the location (1–12) next to the word on the right.

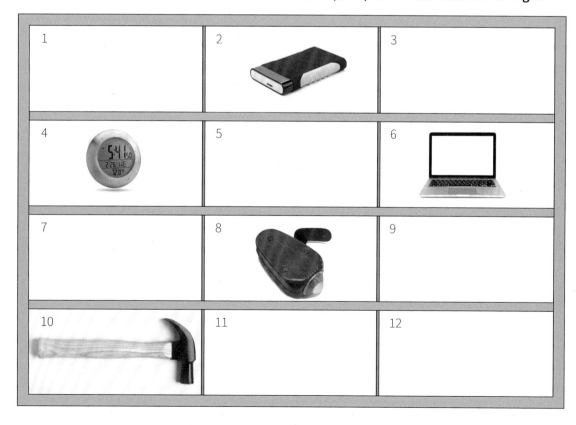

multi-tool ____
pliers ____
radio ____
wrench ____
batteries ____
torch ____
scissors _12_

4 Word list

NOUNS (tools)	NOUNS (electricity)	VERBS	ADJECTIVES
blade	adapter	change	external
bottle opener	alarm	charge	internal
building site	amplifier	connect	plastic
can opener	battery	cut	**PHRASES**
cover	clock	drive in	at the bottom
handle	dynamo	grip	at the top
head	electricity supply	measure	in the centre
jaws	generator	produce	in the middle
key tool	lamp	shine	on the left
metal	mains electricity	turn	on the right
multi tool	radio		above
pick	solar panel		below
pliers	solar power		to the left of
ruler	torch		to the right of
scissors	**NOUNS (computer)**		
shaft	computer		
string	computer station		
survival tool	cursor		
wire	flash drive		
wrench	keyboard		
	mouse		
	printer		
	scanner		
	screen		
	speaker		
	tablet		
	webcam		

1 Match the nouns (1–8) with the phrases (a–h) to make sentences.

1 Chisels
2 Hammers
3 Pliers
4 Rulers
5 Saws
6 Scissors
7 Screwdrivers
8 Wrenches

a) loosen screws.
b) tighten nuts.
c) cut wood into a shape.
d) drive in nails.
e) cut wood or metal.
f) grip wire.
g) measure everything.
h) cut paper.

4 Movement

1 Directions

1 **Look at the pictures (1–4) of the jump jet.**

1 Which picture shows a vertical take-off? (Picture _____)

2 Which picture shows a short take-off? (Picture _____)

3 Which directions can you see? Write the letters from the pictures (A–D) here.

vertically up _____   horizontal _____ diagonally up _____

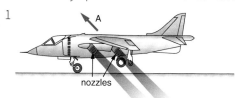

nozzles

2 **Which directions can the jump jet fly? Complete the text with words from the box.**

> forwards   sideways   straight down   ~~straight up~~   to the right   up and down

The jump jet can fly like a helicopter or fly like a passenger plane. The jump jet has one engine and four nozzles. The four nozzles can point straight down. Then the jet engine lifts the plane (1) _straight up_ into the air. In the air, the four nozzles can rotate and point backwards. This pushes the plane (2)_____. Then the plane can fly at about 1165 kph. Like a passenger plane, it can turn to the left or turn (3)_____. It can fly diagonally (4)_____. It can also fly backwards and (5)_____, a little. How does it land? It stops in the air and flies (6)_____.

3 **Read about the movements of the human leg. Complete the text with words from the box.**

> angles   ankle   degrees   directions   hip   knee   move   ~~pivots~~   rotate   sideways

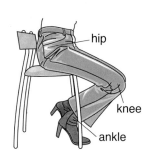

hip

knee

ankle

The leg has three (1) _pivots_, the hip, the knee and the ankle. The ankle can move in three (2)_____. At the (3)_____, the foot can move up and down about 50 (4)_____. It can (5)_____ from side to side about 50 degrees, and it can (6)_____ about 15 degrees. The (7)_____ can move in the same directions, but with different (8)_____. The (9)_____ can only move in one direction. At the knee, the lower leg can only move up and down. It cannot move (10)_____ or rotate.

2 Instructions

1 🔊 4.1 **Write the full forms. Then listen and check.**

1 30 kph   _thirty kilometres per hour_
2 500 rpm   _____
3 15 m/s   _____
4 65 mph   _____
5 8 km/s   _____

2 🔊 4.2 **Listen and write the speeds. Use the short forms from Exercise 1.**

1 Sound travels at _____.
2 The engine of a Formula 1® car turns at about _____.
3 The NASA Mars rover Perseverance travels at _____.
4 A solar-powered car can travel at _____.
5 A person on skis can go downhill at _____.
6 A person on a snowboard can go downhill at _____.
7 The maximum speed of a passenger train in China is _____.
8 The fastest sailing ship sails at _____.
9 A Blackbird jet flies at _____.

3 🔊 4.3 **Listen to the dialogue. Are all the parts for the radio-controlled truck in the box? Listen and tick the things on the list.**

Instruction manual

Transmitter

Truck

Antenna for transmitter

Antenna for truck

Two 9 V batteries

4 **Complete the text about the radio-controlled truck with the correct forms of the verbs in the box.**

| control   move   press   receive   ~~send~~   turn   use |

The transmitter (1)____sends____ radio signals to the receiver in the truck. An antenna on the truck (2)_____ signals from the transmitter. The truck and the transmitter (3)_____ electricity from batteries. Six buttons (4)_____ the speed and direction: forwards, backwards, forwards and left, forwards and right, backwards and left, backwards and right. There are two electric motors. One motor (5)_____ the wheels to the left or right. The other motor drives the back wheels forwards or backwards. (6)_____ the control button 'Forwards'. The motor turns the shaft and the shaft rotates the axle. The truck (7)_____ forward.

1 Read the text from the instruction manual. Write the letters (A–H) from the diagram next to the names of the controls.

The diagram shows the controls of an automatic, right-hand drive car. On the left of the driver's seat is the gear lever (1)_____. Press the button (2)_____ on the gear lever and move it to 'R'; then the car reverses. Press the button and move the gear lever to 'D' and the car moves forwards. In front of the driver's seat is the steering wheel (3)_____. This turns the car to the left or the right. On the left of the steering wheel is a lever. This is the direction indicator (4)_____ for when you turn left or right. Push the lever up and the lights on the right-hand side of the car flash. Push the lever down and the lights on the left-hand side of the car flash. The lever on the right of the steering wheel (5)_____ controls the front lights. Above the floor you can see two pedals. The left-hand pedal is the brake (6)_____. The right-hand pedal is the accelerator (7)_____.

2 Write instructions for driving a car. Write full sentences from these notes. Use *when* and *you*, and add *the* and punctuation.

1   pull gear lever to 'R' → car reverses
    When you pull the gear lever to 'R', the car reverses.

2   pull gear lever to 'D' → car moves forwards
    _____

3   press accelerator → car goes faster
    _____

4   press brake pedal a little → car goes slower
    _____

5   turn steering wheel to the right → car turns right
    _____

6   press brake pedal → car stops
    _____

4 Word list

NOUNS		VERBS	ADVERBS
accelerator	movement	ascend	backwards
angle	parking brake	control	down
antenna	pedal	descend	forwards
brake	pivot	dock	sideways
direction	plane	park	up
display	robot	press	to the left
drone	rotation	pull	to the right
elbow	shoulder	push	**PHRASES**
forearm	steering wheel	reverse	horizontal axis
handle	power switch	rotate	vertical axis
helicopter	tilt	slide	
joystick	transmitter	slow down	
kilometre	wrist	turn round	
lever			
metre			

1 **Find nine nouns for driving a car. Write them here.**

accelerator _____

_____

2 **Find opposites in columns 3 and 4 for the following words and write them here.**

accelerate _____   forwards _____

ascend _____   up _____

pull _____   to the left _____

3 **Find seven verbs in column 3 for flying a helicopter. Write them here.**

Helicopters can accelerate, _____

_____

4 **Look at the diagrams for 'parallel parking' in countries where cars drive on the left. Complete the instructions with adverbs from column 4.**

1   Drive _____ slowly. Stop.

2   Reverse and turn the steering wheel to the _____ .

3   Reverse a little more and turn the steering wheel to the _____ . Stop.

4   Drive _____ a little and turn the steering wheel to the _____ .

Review Unit B

Section 1

1 Look at the diagram of the working-from-home (WFH). workstation. Tick the true statements. Correct the false ones.

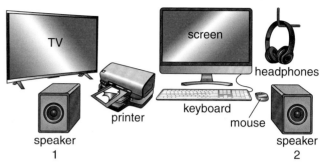

1 The screen is in the centre. ✓_____
2 The keyboard is in the centre, ~~above~~ the screen. _below_____
3 The TV is to the right of the screen. _____
4 The printer is below the screen. _____
5 Speaker 1 is on the right. _____
6 Speaker 2 is on the left. _____
7 The mouse is at the top, to the left of the keyboard. _____
8 The headphones are to the left of the screen, below speaker 1. _____

2 Where are the programmes on the screen? Make sentences with the words in the box.

| ~~bikes~~ cars ~~football~~ the news boats science skateboards space ~~planes~~ |

1 _Football is at the top, on the left._
2 _Planes are at the top, in the centre._
3 _____
4 _Bikes are on the middle line,_
5 _____
6 _____
7 _____
8 _____
9 _____

3 Write the singular form of the words in the box. If a word has no singular form, write a pair of . . .

| ~~batteries~~ hammers ~~overalls~~ pincers pliers scissors spanners wrenches |

1 Singular form: _battery_____ _____ _____
2 No singular form: _a pair of overalls_____
_____ _____

Section 2

1a Match the letters in the diagrams (A–D) with the sentences.

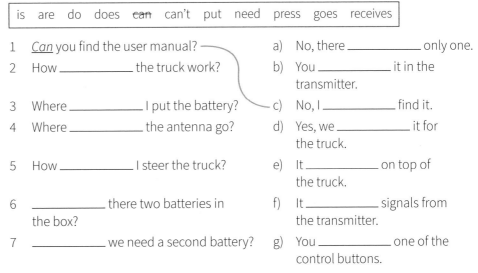

1 (_D_) The crane can move _____ on its wheels.

2 (__) The top part of the crane can _____ through 360°.

3 (__) The arm of the crane can ascend and _____ through 90°.
It can be in a vertical, _____ position.

4 (__) The hook below the end of the arm can go _____.

1b Use the phrases from the box to complete the sentences.

descend   up and down   forwards and backwards   rotate   diagonal or horizontal

2a Use the words in the box to complete these questions and answers.

is   are   do   does   ~~can~~   can't   put   need   press   goes   receives

1 _Can_ you find the user manual?   a) No, there _____ only one.

2 How _____ the truck work?   b) You _____ it in the transmitter.

3 Where _____ I put the battery?   c) No, I _____ find it.

4 Where _____ the antenna go?   d) Yes, we _____ it for the truck.

5 How _____ I steer the truck?   e) It _____ on top of the truck.

6 _____ there two batteries in the box?   f) It _____ signals from the transmitter.

7 _____ we need a second battery?   g) You _____ one of the control buttons.

2b Match the questions with their answers.

3 Read the instructions 1–4 for steering a boat backwards. Then complete them with the following words: *forwards, left, middle, backwards*.

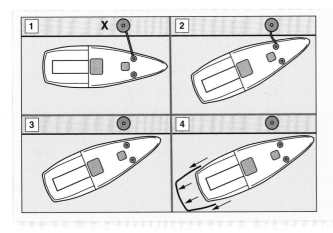

1 Start the engine. Tie the rope on the _____ *left* _____ of the boat to Point X.

2 Turn the steering wheel to the _____ . Push the engine lever forwards; this moves the boat slowly _____ and to the _____ .

3 Pull the engine lever to the _____ position. Loosen the rope. Take the rope off from Point X.

4 Turn the steering wheel to the _____ position. Pull the lever _____ ; this puts the engine into reverse. Reverse slowly.

5 Flow

1 Heating system

1 **Match the words on the top line with their opposites on the bottom line.**

sink above bottom out of cold cool enter outlet push

hot inlet leave heat pull rise top below into

2 **Rewrite the sentences. Change the words in italics. Use words with opposite meanings from Exercise 1.**

1 A solar panel *heats* water. A fridge _cools water._

2 *Hot* water *rises* to the *top* of a water tank.

_____

3 The *inlet* pipe for *cold* water is *below* the pump.

_____

4 Water *enters* the tank through the *inlet* pipe.

_____

5 *Push* the shower head *into* the pipe.

_____

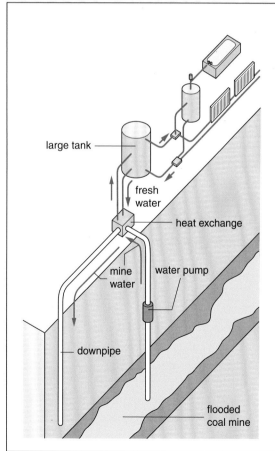

large tank

fresh water

heat exchange

mine water

water pump

downpipe

flooded coal mine

3 **Look at the diagram. Warm water comes up from underground and heats water for the houses. Use the correct forms of the verbs and prepositions in the box to complete the description of the heating system.**

| flow | leave | push | rise | ~~above~~ |
| below | ~~into~~ | through | to | out of |

In this system, there are houses (1) _above_ a flooded coal mine. At 170 metres (2) _____ ground, the temperature of the mine water stays at 14.5 °C.

The water pump brings up the mine water and (3) _____ it (4) _into_ the heat exchanger. The mine water comes (5) _____ the heat exchanger and (6) _____ back into the coal mine (7) _____ the downpipe.

In the heat exchanger, the temperature of the fresh water (8) _____ to 55 °C. This warm water then flows to a large tank. Then it (9) _____ the large tank and goes (10) _____ the houses.

2 Electrical circuit

1 **Match the words in the box with the sentences 1–7.**

battery cable controller ~~lamp~~ solar panel electrical current switch

1 shines a light when the switch is on: _____ *lamp* _____

2 converts the sun's energy into an electrical current: _____

3 stores electricity: _____

4 When a _____ is closed, the electrical current can flow.

5 DC is a type of _____.

6 Electricity passes through the _____ to the lamp or the battery.

7 carries the electrical current: _____

2 🔊 5.1 **Look at the diagram for a waterwheel and a generator which supplies current to a workshop next to the river. Complete the sentences with the present simple. Then listen and check your answers.**

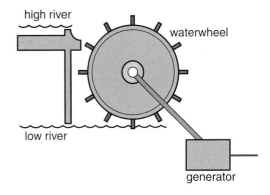

high river

waterwheel

low river

generator

1 If the river is high, and the workshop is open, _*the current flows from the generator*_ _*into the workshop*_. (current / flow / generator / workshop)

2 If the river is high, and the workshop is closed, _____ _____. (current / flow / generator / batteries)

3 If the river is low, and the workshop is open, _____ _____. (current / flow / batteries / workshop)

4 If the river is low, and the workshop is closed, _____ _____. (current / not / flow)

5 If the batteries are full, _____ _____. (current / not / flow / generator / batteries)

6 If the batteries are empty, _____ _____. (current / not / flow / batteries / workshop)

3 🔊 5.2 **Listen to the dialogue. Circle the correct specifications for the items.**

1	Solar panels	a) 4 × 16 W	b) 40 × 60 W	c) 4 × 60 W
2	Controller	a) 1 × 3 A	b) 1 × 5 A	c) 1 × 15 A
3	Batteries	a) 4 × 12 V, 50 Ah	b) 4 × 12 V, 100 Ah	c) 4 × 15 V, 150 Ah
4	Lamps	a) 6 × 20 V, 8 W	b) 16 × 12 V, 18 W	c) 6 × 12 V, 8 W
5	Cable (12 metres)	a) 2.5 mm, 30 amps	b) 6 mm, 53 amps	c) 16 mm, 100 amps

3 Cooling system

1 **Complete these sentences for a world weather forecast. Write the temperatures as words.**

1 The night-time temperature in Helsinki will be _minus two degrees Fahrenheit_. (–2 °F)

2 The day-time temperature in Mexico City will be _twenty-one degrees Celsius_. (21 °C)

3 The day-time temperature in Los Angeles will be

_____. (75 °F)

4 The coldest night-time temperature in Oslo will be

_____. (–8 °C)

5 The day-time temperature in Tunis will be

_____. (24 °C)

6 The highest day-time temperature in Karachi will be

_____. (33 °C)

2 **Use the words in the box to answer the questions with short answers. Use some of the words twice.**

cool water   engine   fan   hot water   thermostat   two hoses   water pump

1 What pushes cool water round the engine? _The water pump_ .

2 What connects the radiator to the engine? _____ .

3 What controls the temperature of the engine? _____ .

4 What flows from the engine to the radiator? _____ .

5 What blows air through the radiator? _____ .

6 What sinks to the bottom of the radiator? _____ .

7 What cools the water in the radiator? _____ .

8 What passes along the bottom hose and back to the engine? _____ .

9 What drives the water pump? _____ .

3 **Look at the diagram for a watering system. Complete the sentences with the words in the box. Put the verbs into the present simple.**

around   at the top   at the bottom   from   into   out of   through

1 From the spring, water ____flows____ (flow) to a reservoir _at the top_ of the hill.

2 _____ the reservoir, water _____ (pass) _____ a pipe to the field.

3 The pipe _____ (go) _____ a field of fruit trees.

4 Water _____ (leave) the pipe _____ small holes.

5 The water then _____ (flow) _____ the fruit trees.

6 A little water _____ (flow) _____ the bottom of the field.

7 This water _____ (enter) a tank _____ of the hill.

spring
reservoir
fruit trees
field
tank

| HEATING AND COOLING | | PREPOSITIONS OF MOVEMENT | ELECTRICAL |
NOUNS	VERBS		NOUNS
engine	blow	around	battery
fan	connect	into	cable
hose	control	out of	conductor
inlet	cool	through	controller
liquid	drive	to	electrical circuit
pump	enter		electrical current
radiator	flow		energy
shower head	go		lamp
solar panel	heat		switch
thermostat	leave		**VERBS**
valve	move		convert
water pipe	pass		shine
water tank	push		short-circuit
	rise		
	sink		

1 Complete the sentences with verbs from column 2.

1   Cold water _____ the system through the inlet.

2   Water _____ into the tank through a pipe.

3   The sun _____ the water in the solar thermal panel.

4   Hot water _____ to the top of the tank.

5   Cold water _____ to the bottom of the tank.

6   Hot water _____ the system through the shower head.

2 Match the sentence halves.

1   The water pump pushes   a)   the temperature of the water.

2   The thermostat controls   b)   air through the radiator.

3   The two hoses connect   c)   the hot water from the engine.

4   The fan blows   d)   water around the engine.

5   The radiator cools   e)   the radiator to the engine.

6 Materials

1 Materials testing

1 Make sentences about the materials with *can . . . , but . . . ,* *can't* or *can . . . and can . . .*

1 (bend / metal / wood) <u>*You can bend metal, but you can't bend wood.*</u>
2 (heat / air / water) <u>*You can heat air and you can heat water.*</u>
3 (melt / plastic / wood) _____
4 (scratch / glass / metal) _____
5 (stretch / nylon / glass) _____
6 (break / glass / wood) _____
7 (cut / wood / metal) _____
8 (compress / air / glass) _____

2 A lecturer is showing a video clip of a test. Complete the description. Use the present continuous.

Hello. Now we can watch the video clip of a car crash. Here they (1) <u>*are testing*</u> (test) the material for the seatbelt. The human dummy (2) _____ (sit) in the test car. This dummy weighs 90 kilos. Here the technician (3) _____ (tighten) the nylon seatbelt around the dummy. Now the technician (4) _____ (start) the engine of the radio-controlled car.

Look at the crash in slo-mo (= slow motion). The car (5) _____ (run) into the concrete block at 40 kph. The body of the dummy (6) _____ (stretch) the nylon seatbelt. And see, the dummy (7) _____ (touch) the airbag. Look carefully. (8) _____ the dummy's face _____ (strike) the front window? No, it isn't. There is no contact with the front window.

3 Write questions and answers for the pictures.

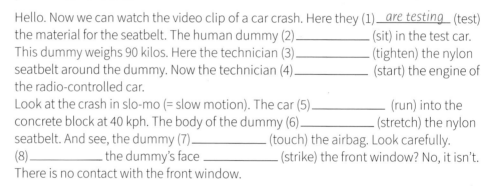

you / push / handles ?
1 **A:** <u>*Are you pushing the handles?*</u>
   B: <u>*No, I'm rowing.*</u>

he / walk ?
2 **A:** _____
   B: _____

she / bend / wall bars ?
3 **A:** _____
   B: _____

you / pull / bar / down ?
4 **A:** _____
   B: _____

she / rotate / legs ?
5 **A:** _____
   B: _____

he / push / bar ?
6 **A:** _____
   B: _____

2 Properties

1 Find the names of 14 materials in the puzzle and circle them. The words go vertically from top to bottom, and sideways from left to right. No words go diagonally.

B	A	J	L	O	Y	C	O	M	P	O	S	I	T	E
P	L	A	S	T	I	C	E	T	O	Z	P	R	A	K
L	U	R	T	I	B	K	Y	L	L	B	O	J	L	I
O	M	A	L	J	M	O	Q	A	Y	U	L	S	D	A
F	I	B	R	E	G	L	A	S	S	I	Y	T	I	Y
B	N	S	D	R	A	R	X	P	T	B	C	N	A	O
T	I	T	A	N	I	U	M	D	Y	F	A	H	M	I
J	U	E	K	Y	L	B	N	T	R	I	R	V	O	Z
A	M	E	B	L	C	B	F	G	E	A	B	H	N	I
J	R	L	K	O	Q	E	S	V	N	U	O	Z	D	W
Y	Z	C	O	N	C	R	E	T	E	X	N	B	G	Y
H	I	R	J	T	K	U	L	C	E	R	A	M	I	C
S	V	N	X	P	G	R	A	P	H	I	T	E	Q	W
I	Y	B	T	L	E	K	O	E	U	J	E	C	D	I

2 Underline the two correct adjectives for each material.

1 A ceramic cup is *flexible / <u>heat-resistant</u>* and <u>*hard*</u> */ soft*.

2 A concrete floor is *rigid / flexible* and *brittle / tough*.

3 A rubber tyre is *rigid / flexible* and *weak / strong*.

4 A fibreglass window frame is *heat-resistant / soft* and *rigid / flexible*.

5 A nylon rope is *rigid / flexible* and *strong / weak*.

6 The graphite in the middle of a pencil is *light / heavy* and *hard / soft*.

7 A polycarbonate road sign is *rigid / flexible* and *strong / weak*.

8 A polystyrene coffee cup is *brittle / tough* and *heavy / light*.

3 Design a plane. Choose one material for each part of the plane.

1 (nose cone / plastic / aluminium)
The nose cone is made of aluminium.

2 (wheels / fibreglass / aluminium alloy)

3 (tyres / ceramic / rubber composite)

4 (frame / composite / polystyrene)

5 (inside / fibreglass / rubber composite)

6 (seats / plastic / ceramic)

7 (engine / fibreglass / aluminium alloy)

8 (wings / aluminium alloy / plastic)

1 🔊 6.1 **Listen and complete the order form. A customer is buying equipment on the phone.**

THE CLIMBING SHOP
ORDER FORM

Date: _23/03/22_

Product name:
_____

Product no:
_____

Quantity:
_____

Colour:
_____

Size:
_____

Material:
_____

Price:
_____

Helmet (polycarbonate/fibreglass)
(L/M/S)

Rope (nylon/nylon + rubber composite)
(50 m / 75 m / 100 m)

Jacket (cotton/polyester)
(XL/L/M/S)

Backpack (nylon/polyester)
(XL/L/M/S)

---

2 🔊 6.2 **Listen and correct the email addresses.**

1   jclark@eyeway.co.uk → _____

2   alex2@antigm.ac.uk → _____

3   s.hagen@whygo.fra → _____

3 🔊 6.3 **Listen and write the website addresses.**

1   News: _____

2   Live radio: _____

3   Radio-controlled toys: _____

4 **A customer is phoning a sports shop. Write questions for the answers.**

1   **Q:** _What's your surname, please?_
    A: It's Badrawi.

2   **Q:** _____
    A: B–A–D–R–A–W–I.

3   **Q:** _____
    A: + 44 1273 497 633.

4   **Q:** _____
    A: Ali dot badrawi at atlas dot com.

5   **Q:** _____
    A: Yes. A–L–I dot badrawi at atlas, that's A–T–L–A–S dot com.

6   **Q:** _____
    A: I need three helmets.

7   **Q:** _____
    A: I'd like white ones, please.

8   **Q:** _____
    A: I want to pay in euros, please.

4 Word list

NOUNS (materials)	NOUNS (car parts, other)	VERBS	ADJECTIVES
alloy	backpack	bend	brittle
aluminium	cone	break	corrosion-resistant
ceramic	engine	burn	flexible
composite	frame	climb	hard
concrete	helmet	coat	heat-resistant
cromoly	jacket	compress	heavy
diamond	piston	corrode	light
fibreglass	radiator	drop	rigid
graphite	rope	heat	soft
nylon	spoiler	hold	strong
plastic	tyre	melt	tough
polycarbonate	vehicle	run	weak
polyester	wheel	scratch	**PHRASES FOR EMAILS**
polystyrene	wing	stretch	
rubber		strike	dash
steel		touch	dot
titanium			

1 Memory test. What is a racing car made of? Write the materials from column 1.

1 The nose cone _is made of fibreglass_____.
2 The wheels _are made of_____.
3 The frame _____.
4 The tyres _____.
5 The radiator _____.
6 The engine _____.
7 The pistons are coated with _____.
8 The wings are made of _____ and
   _____.

2 Write the opposites of the adjectives from the list in column 4.

1 Nylon isn't weak. It's _strong_____.
2 Polystyrene isn't tough. It's _____.
3 Graphite isn't hard. It's _____.
4 Rubber isn't rigid. It's _____.
5 Aluminium isn't heavy. It's _____.

Review Unit C

1 Use the words from the box to complete the phone dialogues.

about   are   here   here   how   I'm   OK   thanks   ~~that~~   this

1   **A:** Hello?
    B: Hello. Is (1) *that* Paulo?
    A: Yes.
    B: It's Sven (2)_____.
    A: Oh, hi, Sven.
    B: Hi. How (3)_____ things?
    A: Great, (4)_____. How are you?
    B: I'm (5)_____.

2   **A:** Hello. Mona Hall (6)_____.
    B: Oh, hi, Mona. (7)_____ is Ingrid.
    A: Hi, Ingrid.
    B: Hi. (8)_____ are you?
    A: Very well. How (9)_____ you?
    B: (10)_____ fine, thanks.

2 Write the *-ing* forms of the verbs on the correct line.

~~bend~~   climb   ~~cut~~   ~~dive~~   drive   drop   grip   heat   hold   leave
move   pull   push   rise   run   sit   strike   swim

1   Add *-ing: bending,* _____

    _____

2   Double the last letter and add *-ing: cutting,* _____

    _____

3   Drop the -e and add *-ing: diving,* _____

    _____

3 Complete the dialogue about the engine's cooling system. Put the verbs into the present continuous. One verb is used twice.

blow   drop   go   push   rise   run   work

A: Is everything OK?

B: No. The engine's cooling system *isn't working.* The temperature of the water _____.

A: _____ the fan _____ air through the radiator?

B: Yes, the fan is fine.

A: _____ the pump _____ water round the engine?

B: Yes, the pump is working.

A: Look! That clip on the bottom hose is loose. Water _____ out of the hose. So the cold water _____ not _____ back to the engine. Tighten the clip. _____ the water _____ out of the hose now?

B: No.

A: Check the temperature.

B: Ah! The temperature _____. Good!

1 **Match phrases from the table to make sentences.**

warm ice cubes	sink
pull a rubber band	burn
strike a ceramic cup very hard	break
heat water to 100 °Celsius	stretch
pour cool water into a radiator	melt
heat pieces of wood	boil

If you warm ice cubes, they melt.

_____

_____

_____

_____

_____

2 **Read the text and complete the table below.**

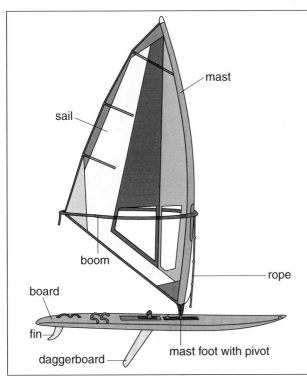

This sailboard is made from light, strong and flexible materials. The board is strong but light. It is made of polystyrene, coated with fibreglass. The mast is strong and flexible. It is made of polycarbonate. The mast and the boom support the sail. The boom is rigid and strong. It is made of aluminium, coated with rubber. The sail is light but strong. It is made of a mixture of nylon and polyester. Fixed to the end of the boom is a strong rope. It is made of nylon. The rigid daggerboard and fin are made of polycarbonate. There is a pivot at the foot of the mast. This is strong and flexible. It is made of rubber.

Part	Material	Properties
board	*polystyrene, fibreglass*	*strong, light*
mast		
boom		
sail		
rope		
daggerboard		
fin		
pivot		

7 Specifications

1 Dimensions

1 **Use the words in the box to label the picture.**

~~bridge~~   cable   deck   pier   pylon   road   span   tunnel

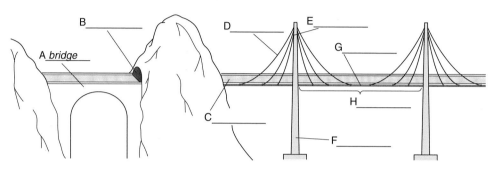

B_____
A *bridge*
D_____   E_____
G_____
C_____
H_____
F_____

2 **Make sentences. Write the words in the correct order.**

1 270 / has / metres / The sea / of / depth / a *The sea has a depth of 270 metres.*

2 deep / is / metres / 25 / river / The _____

3 is / metres / 330 / The / long / span _____

4 160 / The / height / metres / of / have / pylons / a _____
   _____

5 the / 22 / kilometres / length / The / road / of / is _____
   _____

6 width / has / 8 / deck / The / metres / of / a _____

3 **Write questions and answers about the bridge.**

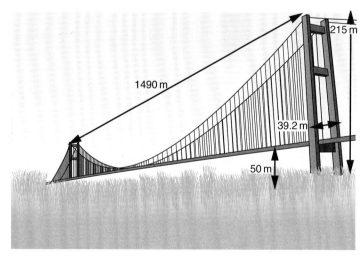

1490 m
215 m
39.2 m
50 m

Runyang Bridge, China

1 where / this bridge ?
   Q: *Where is this bridge?*
   A: *It's in China.*

2 long / inner span ?
   Q: _____
   A: _____

3 high / pylons ?
   Q: _____
   A: _____

4 wide / deck ?
   Q: _____
   A: _____

5 high / deck / above water ?
   Q: _____
   A: _____

1 **Complete the text with facts from the specification chart.**

The Gherkin

Address: 30 St Mary Axe, London
Completion date: 2003
Height: 180 m
Floors: 40
Glass area: 24 000 sq m
Floor area: circle
Footprint: small
Number of lifts: 18
Speed of lifts: 6 m/s
Materials: reinforced concrete, steel, aluminium, glass
Width of glass lens: 2.4 metres

This building is called 'The Gherkin'. It was completed in (1) __2003__ . The
(2)_____-storey building is 180 (3)_____ high. The building is made of
(4)_____, (5)_____, (6)_____ and (7)_____. The glass windows have
an (8)_____ of 24 000 (9)_____. The building has (10)_____ lifts. Each lift
travels at 6 (11)_____. Each floor area of the building is a (12)_____. The floors
at the top and bottom are small. The floors in the middle of the building are bigger.
The footprint of the building is (13)_____. All the glass on the side of the building
is flat. But on the top of the building, there is one round glass lens. It is 2.4 metres
(14)_____.

2 **🔊 7.1 A customer is ordering some materials. Listen and complete the order form.**

Item	Kind (circle)	Size (circle)	Product number (circle)	Quantity (write)
Paint	green / grey	5 / 10 litre tin	P176GR / D186G	
Cement	grey / white	10 / 20 kg bag	C0116W / S0196G	
Nails	packet of 50 / 100	24 / 30 mm	N420 / N240	
Screws	packet of 50 / 100	20 / 24 mm	S00941 / F00921	

3 **🔊 7.2 Listen and complete the questions from Exercise 2.**

1 _How much paint_____ do you need?
2 _____ _____ _____ do you need?
3 _____ _____ _____ do you need?
4 _____ _____ _____ do you need?
5 _____ _____ _____ do you need?
6 Do you have _____ _____?
7 _____ _____ _____ do you need?
8 Do you need _____ _____?

3 Future projects

1 Read the article about a train tunnel. Complete the Technical Overview below.

The Brenner Base Tunnel

The Brenner Base Tunnel (BBT) will be the second longest railway tunnel in the world. It will run from Austria under the Eastern Alps into Italy. Engineers are building it now and will finish the project in 2032.

Today, many trucks use the roads over the Alps. In future, they will use the BBT. The tunnel will connect Innsbruck in Austria to Fortezza in Italy.

There will be two tunnels. Each tunnel will be about 55 km long. They will reach a height of 794 metres above sea level. The new trains will use electricity. Some trains will carry goods. Fast passenger trains will travel at 250 kph. About 400 trains per day will use the BBT.

Brenner Base Tunnel (BBT)	
Location of tunnel	*between Austria and Italy*
Completion date	
Number of tunnels	
Length of tunnels	
Height above sea level	
Maximum speed of trains	
Source of power for trains	
Number of trains per day	

2 Change the long forms to short forms.

1 They are building a new tunnel. *They're building a new tunnel.*
2 There will be two new tunnels. _____
3 They will finish the tunnel in 2032. _____
4 The trains will not use magnetism. _____
5 There will be about 400 trains per day. _____

3 Underline seven mistakes in this report. Then rewrite the report.

> The BBT will be the second longest <u>road</u> tunnel in the world. It will connect Italy and France. Engineers will finish the project in 2030. The new tunnel will be about 790 metres below sea level. There will be about 400 trains per week. The new trains will use diesel. All of them will run at 250 kph.

The GBT will be the second longest railway tunnel _____
_____
_____

NOUNS (bridge)	NOUNS (design)	NOUNS (materials)	VERBS
cable	completion	aluminium	attach
deck	depth	cement	build
pier	design	fibreglass	fix
pylon	elevator	glass	lay
span	footprint	glue	make
NOUNS (tunnel)	foundation	oil	put
compressed air	height	paint	**ADJECTIVES**
diesel	length	reinforced concrete	amazing
magnetism	location	steel	approximate
vacuum	material	superglue	deep
	quantity	**NOUNS (units)**	high
	shape	bag	inner
	specification	bottle	long
	storey	cubic metre	outer
	structure	packet	super-fast
	width	tin	wide
		tube	Y-shaped

1 **Find nouns for these adjectives in the NOUNS (design) column in the Word list.**

long – l_____   high – h_____   wide – w_____   deep – d_____

2 **Make phrases from the words in the box. Write them below.**

a	bottle tube bag packet tin	of	cement oil paint glue / superglue screws

_____   _____

_____   _____

_____

3 **Choose a verb from the VERBS column in the Word list and complete these phrases. One verb is used twice.**

1 *lay* the foundations
2 _____ the piers
3 _____ the pylons on the piers
4 _____ the cables to the pylons
5 _____ the deck
6 _____ the deck to the cables
7 _____ the road

Reporting

1 Recent incidents

1 Complete the table of verb forms.

		Verb	Past simple	Past participle
Type A Regular	add *-ed*	*check*		
	add *-d*			*changed*
Type B Regular	double the final letter and add *-ed*		*stopped*	
Type C Irregular	verb = past simple = past participle	*cut*		
Type D Irregular	past simple = past participle		*bought*	
				sold
Type E Irregular	past simple ≠ past participle		*fell*	
		speak		
				taken

2 Complete the dialogue. A is the manager and B is the manager's assistant.

THINGS TO DO

speak to Security ✓

ring the new customer

send an email to HTB ✓

write incident report

A: <u>Have you spoken</u> _____ to Security?

B: Yes, I have.

A: Good. _____ the new customer?

B: No, I haven't. I'll do it now.

A: _____ an email to HTB?

B: Yes, _____.

A: Good. _____the incident report?

B: No, _____. I'll do it now.

3 Yesterday, the police received a lot of phone calls. Complete the sentences with the present perfect form of the verbs in brackets and the nouns from the box.

| diamonds ~~digger~~ motor boat shop river town centre shop window sledgehammer |

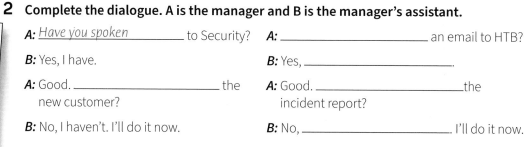

1 Hello? Police? A thief <u>has taken</u> my <u>digger</u>. (take)

2 Police? A man _____ (drive) a digger into the _____ here.

3 Hello? A digger _____ (crash) into a _____ in Broad Street.

4 Help! Two men _____ (come) into my _____ in Broad Street.

5 One man _____ (break) the display case with a _____.

6 The two thieves _____ (steal) some _____.

7 Two men with bags _____ (run) down to the _____.

8 The two men _____ (jump) into a _____. They are on the river now.

2   Damage and loss

1   🔊 8.1   **Fill in the gaps and underline the best verbs. Then listen, check and repeat.**

1   They ___have___ _bent_ / _burnt_ the router antenna.

2   The user manual ___is___ _torn_ / _burnt_.

3   Someone _____ _bent_ / _broken_ the camera.

4   The body of the radio _____ _cracked_ / _cut_.

5   The speakers _____ _damaged_ / _torn_.

6   Someone _____ _cut_ / _bent_ the power cable.

7   The lenses of the goggles _____ _cut_ / _scratched_.

8   I _____ _burnt_ / _broken_ my overalls.

9   They _____ _dented_ / _torn_ the car door.

2   🔊 8.2   **Listen to Part 1 of the dialogue and correct the customer details.**

Order No:	PC08/1020/0017	Item	Damaged	Missing
Name:	Mr ~~Bert~~ Sandle _Burt_	1 router antenna	_bent_	
Address:	14 Hayford Road	2 mouse		✓
	Catford	3 computer screen		
	London	4 keyboard		
Postcode:	SE10 4QU	5 power cable		
Tel:	0208 411 4009	6 LH speaker		
Email:	bsandell87@bdg.co.uk	7 RH speaker		
		8 user manual		

3   🔊 8.3   **Listen to Part 2 of the dialogue and complete the damage report in Exercise 2.**

4   **Complete the sentences. Some of the phrases are used more than once.**

> are   doesn't have   has   is   there's   there are

Reporting damage	Reporting something missing
1 The box ___is___ damaged.	1 The headphones _____ missing.
2 The overalls _____ torn.	2 _____ no pliers in the toolbox.
3 _____ a dent on one of the speakers.	3 The power cable _____ a plug.
4 _____ some cracks on the radio.	4 The radio _____ no antenna.
	5 _____ no user manual in the box.

1 Read the diary of a space tourist. Then complete the interview below.

> 12.04.22 Took off on Soyuz rocket. Took 6 Luka cameras and laptop.
>
> 13.04.22 Rocket docked with International Space Station (ISS)
>
> 14.04.22 Tested all 6 Luka cameras. All worked OK.
>
> 15.04.22 John did spacewalk. He repaired solar panel on ISS.
>
> 20.04.22 Left ISS, after 7 days.
>
> 21.04.22 Returned to Earth. Landed in Kazakhstan.

1   **Q:**   which year / travel / to / ISS?
        Which year did you travel to the ISS?

     A: In 2022.

2   **Q:**   when / you / take off ?

     A: On the 12th of April.

3   **Q:**   how / travel / into space ?

     A: On a Soyuz rocket.

4   **Q:**   what / take / with you ?

     A: Six Luka cameras and my laptop.

5   **Q:**   what / do / on / ISS ?

     A: I tested all the Luka cameras.

6   **Q:**   you / repair / solar panel ?

     A: No. John repaired it.

7   **Q:**   when / you / leave / ISS ?

     A: On the 20th of April.

8   **Q:**   when / you / return / Earth ?

     A: On the 21st of April.

2 Ben damaged his laptop a month ago. He rang the IT hotline. Write his answers to the questions. Use the past simple + *ago*.

1   When did you buy your laptop? (10 months)
     I bought it 10 months ago.

2   When did you drop it? (4 weeks)

3   When did you bring it into the Service Department? (10 days)

4   When did you send your email? (3 days)

4 Word list

VERBS (irregular)	VERBS (regular)	NOUNS (general)	NOUNS (building)
bend / *bent*	check	accident	beam
break	crack	ambulance	brick
burn	crash	body (of radio)	bucket
buy	dent	carrying bag	builder
cut	drop	charging cable	crane
drive	happen	controller	digger
fall	land	damage	hard hat
go	launch	display screen	scaffolding
lose	move	fuse	sledgehammer
put	order	goggles (plural)	**NOUNS (space)**
sell	raise	headset	global navigation
send	repair	insulation	moon
speak	**VERBS (damage)**	lens	satellite
steal	bend	overalls (plural)	shuttle
take	break	spark plug	space station
tear	burn	strap	space walk
write	crack	surface	telescope
PHRASAL VERBS	cut	VR headset	
pick up (regular)	dent		
put on (irregular)	scratch		
take off (irregular)	tear		

1 Write the past tenses of all the irregular verbs on the Word list. (See the example at the top of column 1.)

2 Complete the sentences with nouns from the Word list.

1 They put the i_____ around the water pipe.
2 She climbed up to the top of the s_____.
3 He broke the bricks with a s_____.
4 He put a h_____ h_____ on his head and started work.
5 The c_____ lifted the metal beam onto the building.
6 One of the builders drove the d_____ into a brick wall.
7 She didn't put on her g_____ and damaged her eyes.
8 She stopped work, took off her dirty o_____ and went home.

Review Unit D

1 Use the words and phrase in the box to complete the texts. Some are used more than once.

at	below	deep	depth	length	long	more than	through	wide	width

The Corinth Canal

The Corinth Canal is in Greece. It is 6.8 kilometres (1)_____ and 21 metres (2)_____. The (3)_____ of the water in the canal is 8 metres. Large ships cannot sail (4)_____ the canal, but small tourist ships can. (5)_____ 11 000 ships travel through the canal every year.

The TauTona Gold Mine

The TauTona gold mine is in South Africa. It has a maximum (6)_____ of 3.5 km. The total (7)_____ of tunnels is (8)_____ 800 km. Mine workers get to the bottom of the mine in super-fast lifts. These travel (9)_____ 16 m/s. The mine opened in 1957. Soon they will open a new mine. This will be 3.9 km (10)_____.

The Channel Tunnel

The Channel Tunnel is a railway tunnel between England and France. It has two tunnels for trains. Each tunnel is 51.5 km (11)_____ and 7.7 metres (12)_____. There is a small third tunnel for engineers. This has a (13)_____ of 4.8 metres. The under-sea part of the tunnel has a (14)_____ of 39 km. Most of the tunnel is 45 metres (15)_____ the sea floor. The travel time (16)_____ the tunnel is 20 minutes. Tunnels were started in 1881 and in 1922. The present tunnel was completed in 1994.

2 Use the words in the box to complete the dialogues.

any	how	many	many	much	one	six	~~some~~	some

1 **A:** Hello. Can I help you?

  B: Yes. I'm building a wall and I need ___*some*___ cement.

  A: _____ much do you need?

  B: I need two bags, please. And I also need _____ sand.

  A: How _____ bags do you need?

  B: I need _____ bags, please.

2 **A:** Hello. What can I do for you?

  B: Do you have _____ paint?

  A: Yes. How _____ do you need?

  B: 10 litres, please. And I need some nails.

  A: How _____ packets?

  B: _____ packet, please.

1 Complete the table.

Verb	Past simple	Past participle
bend	*bent*	*bent*
build		
burn		
find		
lose		
pay		
break	*broke*	*broken*
come		
give		
go		

2 Ask questions about these recent incidents. Use the words in brackets.

1 A digger has driven into a shop window. (when / the / the)
   When did the digger drive into the shop window?

2 Some thieves have broken into the office. (when / the)
   _____

3 A mechanic has found some money. (how much / the)
   _____

4 Some builders have taken off the old roof. (when / the)
   _____

5 Some scaffolding has fallen down. (where / the)
   _____

3 Complete the dialogue. A is the supervisor and B is the builder. They are discussing things to do next week.

A: Have you put up the scaffolding?

B: Yes, I have.

A: Good. Have you changed the power cable?

B: No, I haven't. I'll do it next week.

A: _____

B: _____

A: _____

B: _____

A: _____

B: _____

THINGS TO DO
put up scaffolding ✓
change the power cable ✗
buy the bricks ✗
speak to the supplier ✓
order the water tank ✗

1 Operation

1 Use the words in the box to complete the text.

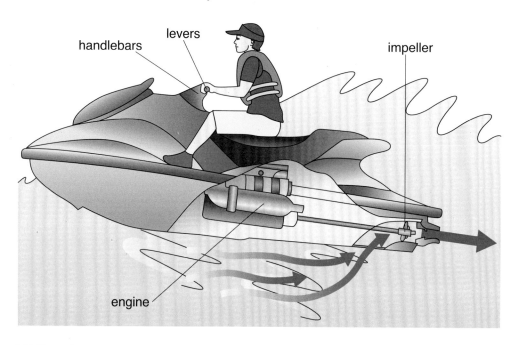

handlebars   levers   impeller   engine

| controls | drives | propels | pulls | pushes | release | steers | ~~supports~~ |

Personal watercraft

A personal watercraft has a fibreglass body and an engine. A seat is mounted on the body and (1) _supports_ the rider. The rider (2)_____the craft with handlebars and (3)_____ the speed with levers. The engine is mounted on the body of the craft and (4)_____ the impeller. The impeller (5)_____ water in and (6)_____ it out. This (7)_____ the craft forwards. If you want to stop the craft, you (8)_____ the lever. This stops the engine.

2 Complete the questions and answers.

1 What ___does___ the engine do?   It _____.
2 What _____ the impeller do?   It _____.
3 What _____ the handlebars do?   They _____.
4 What _____ the levers do?   _____
5 What _____ the seat _____?   _____

3 Make sentences with the words. Use *mounted on* or *attached to*.

1 seat / body   _The seat is mounted on the body._
2 handlebars / body   _____
3 levers / handlebars   _____
4 engine / body   _____

2 Hotline

1 **Find these things in the working-from-home (WFH) office. Write the words below.**

| adapter | printer | ~~display~~ | mouse | power switch | speaker |

1 _display_   3 _____   5 _____

2 _____   4 _____   6 _____

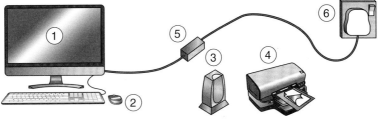

2 **Look at the picture in Exercise 1. Correct these sentences.**

1 The display is off. → _The display_ _____ .

2 The power switch is up. → _____

3 The computer is disconnected. → _____

4 The printer is off. → _____

3 🔊 9.1 **Listen to three dialogues between a customer and a technician. What was the problem in each dialogue? Underline your answers.**

Dialogue 1: The computer *was / wasn't* plugged in. The adapter *was / wasn't* connected to a power source.

Dialogue 2: The adapter *was / wasn't* connected to a power source. The speaker *was / wasn't* connected to the adapter.

Dialogue 3: The display *was / wasn't* working. / The mouse battery *was / wasn't* charged.

4 🔊 9.2 **Use the words in the box to complete the dialogues. Then listen and check.**

| is | isn't | are | aren't | does | doesn't | do | don't |

1 *Does* the computer start?
No, it _____ .
Right. Press the power button again.

2 _____ the power switch down?
No, it _____ .
OK. Press it down.

3 _____ the loudspeakers connected?
No, they _____ .
OK. Connect them.

4 _____ the adapter connected?
Yes, it _____ .
Good.

5 _____ the loudspeakers work?
No, they _____ .
OK. Connect them and try again.

6 _____ the two LED lights on?
Yes, they _____ .
Good.

7 _____ the computer start?
Yes, it _____ .
Good.

8 _____ the loudspeakers work now?
Yes, they _____ .
Good.

3 User guide

1 Read the Troubleshooting Guide. Underline the correct words.

> ## Travelling with your notebook computer
>
> *Close / Open* the display.
> *Press / Turn* the power button.
> If the display light is low, *check / replace* the LED for the battery.
> If the battery is low, *connect / recharge* it.
> If the battery still doesn't *work / start*, replace it.
> At the end, to turn off your computer, *release / press* the power button.
> *Close / Open* the display.

2 Make sentences with *if* from the dialogues.

1 Are the LEDs on? No, they aren't. OK. Check the battery.	3 Is the printer light on? No, it isn't. OK. Push the 'On' button.	5 Do the speakers work? No, they don't. OK. Connect them to a power source.
2 Does the printer work? No, it doesn't. OK. Connect it to the adapter.	4 Are the batteries old? Yes, they are. OK. Replace them.	6 Does it print in black? Yes, it does. OK. Press the button for 'Colour'.

1 *If the LEDs aren't on, check the battery.*

2 _____

3 _____

4 _____

5 _____

6 _____

3 Use verbs from the box to complete the Troubleshooting Guide.

> ~~check~~ check connected plug ~~plugged~~ press press shut shuts turns unplug

(1) _____*Check*_____ that the power cable is (2) _____*plugged*_____ into the computer and a power outlet.
(3) _____ that the mouse and the keyboard are (4) _____. Unplug the cables and then (5) _____ them in again.
(6) _____ the power button on the back of the computer for a few seconds. This (7) _____ down the computer.
If you cannot (8) _____ down the computer, (9) _____ the power cable from the computer. Wait 30 seconds. Plug it back in. (10) _____ the power button. This (11) _____ the computer on.

4 Word list

NOUNS		VERBS	ADJECTIVES
acceleration	hovercraft	accelerate	connected
adapter	hub	check	fibreglass
airboard	key	connect	flat
battery	LED	contain	flexible
body	lever	control	open
brake	notebook computer	drive	rubber
cable socket	platform	force	**PREPOSITIONS**
circuit	power button	hold	above
computer	powerline adapter	increase	attached **to**
current	power outlet	open	below
cushion	power source	press	connected **to**
diagram	purpose	propel	mounted **on**
display	rider	recharge	suspended **from**
engine	router	release	**PHRASES**
fan	satellite dish	replace	pull (air) in
friction wheel	screen	start	push (air) out
front	skirt	steer	suck (air) in)
function	speaker	stop	switch off
games console	speed	support	switch on
handlebar	starter motor	touch	You're welcome.
HDMI cable	switch	turn	
hotline		**ADVERBS**	
		backwards	
		downwards	
		forwards	
		upwards	

1 **Find 20 nouns that are connected to computers.**

_____

_____

2 **Replace the underlined words with opposites from columns 3 and 4 of the Word list.**

1   The rider <u>presses</u> the lever.   →   _The rider releases the lever._____

2   The fan <u>pushes</u> air <u>out</u>.   →   _____

3   The rider can go <u>forwards</u>.   →   _____

4   The engine is <u>above</u> the platform.   →   _____

_____

5   The fan <u>starts</u> and the airboard goes <u>upwards</u>.   →

_____

10 Safety

1 Rules and warnings

1 Label the objects with these words.

| safety boots | safety goggles | safety gloves | safety helmet |

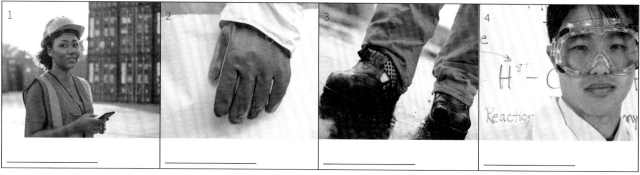

1 _____

2 _____

3 _____

4 _____

2 Use the words in the box to complete the instructions. Some words are used more than once.

| always | do | don't | must | mustn't | never |

1 ___*Don't*___ smoke in the workshop.

2 _____ use mobile phones in the workshop.

3 You _____ wear safety goggles when you use this machine.

4 You must _____ enter the cold store if you are alone in the factory.

5 _____ not lift heavy weights by hand.

6 You _____ use this machine without the guard.

7 _____ read the manual before you service the machine.

8 _____ touch packets in the cold store without gloves.

3 Complete each sentence with a pair of verbs.

| ~~drop~~ / ~~break~~ | lift / hurt | pick / burn | put / melt |
| touch / get | use / scratch | use / trap | |

1 Don't ___*drop*___ that box. You might ___*break*___ the TV inside it.

2 Don't _____ the DVD on that hot surface. It could _____.

3 Don't _____ that box without a forklift truck. You might _____ your back.

4 Don't _____ a hook when you lift the car. You might _____ it.

5 Don't _____ up that hot plate. You might _____ your hand.

6 Don't _____ that wire. You could _____ an electric shock.

7 Don't _____ that machine without a guard. You could _____ your hand in it.

2 Safety hazards

1 An inspector is inspecting a factory. Write sentences from her notes.

1 liquid on floor *There is some liquid on the floor.*

2 hole in the outside door _____

3 no fire exit _____

4 broken window _____

5 cables on a workbench _____

6 no fire extinguishers in factory _____

7 two machine guards missing _____

8 some damaged warning cones _____

2 Use phrases from the box with *might* or *could* to complete these warnings.

burn your hand   fall into it   get an electric shock   injure your head   start a fire   trap your hair in it   trip over them

1 Mind that lighted match! _____*You could start a fire.*_____ (could)

2 Mind that cable! _____ (might)

3 Mind those bricks! _____ (could)

4 Mind that machine! It doesn't have a guard.
_____ (might)

5 Mind the gap! _____ (could)

6 Mind that low beam! _____ (might)

7 Mind that circular saw! It's very hot. _____
(could)

3 Complete the inspector's report about the hazards in a factory. Use each of the words or phrases once.

there was   ~~there were~~   was   were   two   no   some   the

1 *There* ___*were*___ no fire extinguishers anywhere in the factory.

2 There was _____ food and drink on the workbenches.

3 There _____ some boxes of parts on the stairs.

4 _____ guard on one of the machines was broken.

5 _____ some oil on the floor.

6 _____ of the windows were broken.

7 The fire exit _____ locked with a padlock.

8 There was _____ key for the padlock.

1 🔊 10.1 **Listen to the dialogue. Complete the details on the accident report form.**

About the accident	Type of accident (tick)	About the injured person
Date: _____ Time: _____ Location: _____ _____	[ ] injured self [ ] injured somebody else [ ] slipped, tripped or fell [ ] lifted something [ ] dropped something	Name: _____ Job title: _____ Injury: _____ _____ At work: Yes / No (circle)

2 🔊 10.2 **Listen to the questions from Exercise 1. Complete the questions that you hear.**

1 First, __*where*__ did the accident __*happen*__ ?

2 Was _____ hurt?

3 When did it _____ _____?

4 What's the name of the _____ person?

5 What _____ he _____?

6 What's his _____?

7 Did he injure _____ _____?

8 What _____?

3 **Read the newspaper story. Complete it with the words from the box.**

away   between   in   in   into   into   of   ~~on~~   on   on   on   out   with

SIX FISHERMEN RESCUED

(1) On 19 March, there was an accident (2)_____ the North Sea. A cargo ship crashed (3)_____ the fishing boat *Marianna*. The accident happened in the North Sea (4)_____ dense fog, 300 kilometres east (5)_____ Hull. The cargo ship was (6)_____ a journey from Sweden to Portugal (7)_____ a cargo of 2000 tons of wood. The *Marianna* was (8)_____ its way back to Hull, after a four-day fishing trip. There were six fishermen on it. The captain said later: 'The warning system on our boat switched (9)_____ automatically. Suddenly, I saw the Swedish cargo ship. The distance (10)_____ us was only 30 metres. I tried to steer our ship (11)_____ from it. But it hit us and our boat sank. We launched our life raft, got (12)_____ it and sent (13)_____ a radio signal for help. We were in our life-raft for four hours.'

4 Word list

NOUNS		VERBS	PHRASAL VERBS
altitude	match	coil	look out
aviation	padlock	hurt	take care
chemical	poison	injure	take place
cone	prohibition	investigate	**ADJECTIVES**
distance	runway	land (a plane)	bare
drink	safety	light	careful
factory	shock	lock	circular
flight	sign	prohibit	mandatory
food	site	service	parallel
gap	surface	slip	round
gear	type	touch	single
glove	warning	trap	triangular
guard	weight	trip	
hazard	**COMPOUND NOUNS**	warn	
high-voltage	fire exit	wash	
hook	fire extinguisher	wear	
incident	mobile phone		
investigation	near miss		
laser			
liquid			
machine			

1 Write adjectives to complete these phrases from the unit.

1 _dense_ cloud
2 b_____ hand
3 l_____ match
4 n_____ miss
5 c_____ saw
6 e_____ shock
7 h_____-voltage

2 Complete these compound nouns from the unit.

1 _____fire_____ extinguisher
2 s_____ boot
3 s_____ hazard
4 s_____ level
5 f_____ path
6 m_____ phone
7 b_____ site

3 Find eight nouns and compound nouns in the Word list that come from the story and report on page 78 of the Course Book. Write them here.

altitude, _____

_____

Review Unit E

Section 1

1 **Complete the description with the nouns in the box.**

> acceleration   body   ~~cushion~~   engines   fans
> fibreglass   levers   platform   skirt

An Air Cushion Vehicle (ACV), or hovercraft, moves over land and water on a
(1) _____cushion_____ of air. Two powerful (2) _____ drive two large (3) _____.
They suck the air in and push the air downwards under the rubber (4) _____.
The engines are mounted on a strong (5) _____. The (6) _____ of the
hovercraft is made of foam covered with (7) _____. Two (8) _____ next to
the driver's seat control the speed of the fans and the (9) _____ of the hovercraft.

2 **Complete the dialogue with a hotline technician. Use the words in the box.
Use some of the words more than once.**

> can
> does
> doesn't
> have
> haven't
> is
> I've
> there's

Technician: Printer Hotline. How (1) _____can_____ I help you?

Customer: I've got a problem with my printer. It (2) _____ work.
(3) _____ switched it on, but (4) _____ no light on the display.

Technician: OK. First, (5) _____ the printer connected to the AC adapter?

Customer: Yes, it (6) _____.

Technician: Good. And (7) _____ you connected the adapter to the power
source?

Customer: Yes, I (8) _____.

Technician: And (9) _____ you turned the switch on?

Customer: Ah, no, I (10) _____. I'll do that now.

Technician: And (11) _____ the printer work now?

Customer: Yes, it (12) _____. Thanks.

3 **Look at the flow chart for a personal watercraft. Use the chart to complete the
Troubleshooting Guide.**

> Turn the key to the right and press _____. If the engine starts,
> move _____ and _____. If the engine
> _____. If the battery _____. If the
> battery _____. If the battery still _____.

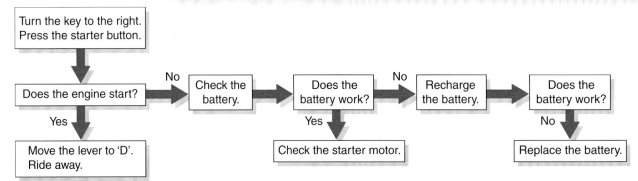

Turn the key to the right.
Press the starter button.

Does the engine start?   **No** →   Check the
battery.   →   Does the
battery work?   **No** →   Recharge
the battery.   →   Does the
battery work?

Yes ↓

Move the lever to 'D'.
Ride away.

Yes ↓ (battery work)

Check the starter motor.

No ↓ (battery work)

Replace the battery.

1 **Write these words in the correct order to make safety signs.**

1 use / after / this / machine / Turn off → _Turn off_ _____.

2 the shipyard / in / boots / safety / Always use → _____

3 report / to / Drivers / must / the office → _____

4 the / truck / Never ride / forklift / on → _____

5 safety goggles / Do not / without / this machine / use → _____

6 a supervisor / reverse / without / You / must not → _____

2 **Complete the safety report with the correct form of the verbs in brackets.**

Moderna Shipyard

On 13 May, I (1) _inspected_ (inspect) the Moderna shipyard. I (2) _____ (find) a number of safety hazards. There (3) _____ (be) some tools on the ground. There (4) _____ (be) some wire coiled outside the office. Eight of the workers (5) _____ (not have) hard hats. There (6) _____ (be) no safety signs.

In April, there (7) _____ (be) a serious incident in the shipyard. Two ships (8) _____ (be) in the shipyard. A crane (9) _____ (lift) a metal beam from one of the ships into the air. But there (10) _____ (be) no rope attached to the beam. The beam (11) _____ (come) downwards. But it (12) _____ (move) in the air and (13) _____ (hit) a forklift truck. The top of the forklift truck (14) _____ (be) bent. The driver was lucky. Just before the accident, another worker (15) _____ (shout), 'Mind your head!' The driver of the forklift truck (16) _____ (see) the beam and he (17) _____ (not be) hurt.

3 **Write questions for these answers about the incident in Exercise 2.**

1 **Q:** (Where / incident) _Where did the incident happen?_ _____
  A: It happened in the shipyard.

2 **Q:** (When / take place) _____
  A: It took place in April.

3 **Q:** (take place / on a ship) _____
  A: No. It took place near a ship, under a crane.

4 **Q:** (What / crane / lift) _____
  A: It lifted a metal beam from the ship.

5 **Q:** (there / rope / attached / to the beam) _____
  A: No, there wasn't.

6 **Q:** (beam / hit / worker) _____
  A: No. It hit his forklift truck.

7 **Q:** (worker / hurt) _____
  A: No, he wasn't hurt.

11 Cause and effect

1 Pistons and valves

1 Complete the description of a dual-flush toilet with words from the diagrams.

half-flush button   full-flush button

fill valve   flush valve
float cable

tank

inlet pipe   rubber seal

The toilet has two buttons on the top of the (1) _tank;_ the (2) _____ releases three litres, and the (3) _____ releases six litres. Less water is needed to flush liquid waste; more water is needed to flush solid waste.

Inside the tank are two valves, the (4) _____ and the flush valve. After the toilet is flushed, water starts to flow along the (5) _____ , through the fill valve and into the tank. Inside the top of the fill valve, there is a (6) _____ . As the water level rises, the float rises too. When it reaches its set level, it stops the inflow of water.

To flush the toilet, press the large or the small flush button. This is connected to a (7) _____ , which pulls up the (8) _____ (a type of drop-valve). Water then flows through the flush valve and down into the (9) _____ . As soon as the tank is empty, the flush valve drops down onto its (10) _____ .

2 Tick the correct forms for the verbs.

	. . . it do	. . . it to do	. . . it (from) doing
allow		✓	
cause			
let / make			
prevent / stop			

3 Rewrite these sentences to give similar meanings. Replace the verbs in italics with the correct form of the verbs in brackets.

1 The pump *makes* the water flow along the pipes.
   The pump causes _____ (cause)

2 The valves *allow* air to enter the tyres.
   _____ (let)

3 The valves *don't let* air escape from the tyres.
   _____ (prevent)

4 The sun *causes* the solar panel to heat the water.
   _____ (make)

5 The cooling system *doesn't allow* the engine to get very hot.
   _____ (stop)

6 The closed inlet valve *prevents* the water from flowing out.
   _____ (not allow)

2 Switches and relays

1 Complete the description of a circuit breaker with words from the diagram. Some words are used more than once, e.g. *switch* (three times).

fixed contact

terminal

switch

moving contact

catch

electromagnet

terminal

A circuit breaker has a (1) ___*switch*___ on the outside of the box. You can turn this on or off. When the (2)_____ is up (on), electricity flows into the circuit breaker through the bottom (3)_____. It flows through the (4)_____. It then flows up to the (5)_____ and across to the (6)_____. Then the electricity flows out of the circuit breaker at the top (7)_____.

If the electrical current jumps to a dangerous level, the electromagnet pulls down a (8)_____. This pulls the (9)_____ away from the (10)_____. This breaks the circuit. At the same time, the (11)_____ drops to the 'down' position. The electricity is now shut off.

2 Read the three texts below. Write the titles above the texts.

a) Emergency exit   b) Home security   c) Car security

1 _____

This security system uses a metal ball inside a metal pipe. When the ball remains still, it touches two of the electrical contacts. This completes the electrical circuit. If the ball moves, it breaks the circuit and opens a switch. If somebody makes the car move, the system causes the horn to sound. It makes the car lights go on too. If somebody hits the car a few times, it makes the siren sound.

2 _____

The ExitGuard is mounted over the door handle. It has a battery-operated alarm. When somebody breaks open the ExitGuard, this causes the alarm to sound. The ExitGuard allows shops to secure their emergency exits. This stops people from using the exits to enter the shop. But it lets people leave the shop in an emergency.

3 _____

If you keep expensive equipment in your workshop, fit a burglar alarm. When the doors and windows of the workshop are shut, the electrical switches are closed. This allows electricity to flow around the electrical circuit. If a burglar forces open a window or door, this breaks the circuit. This causes the burglar alarm to sound. If your workshop is a long distance away, install the alarm buzzer inside your house. This allows you to hear the alarm inside your house.

3 Read the texts in 2 again and mark the sentences (1–6) *T* (true) or *F* (false). Correct the false parts of the sentences.

1   Two of the systems cause an alarm to sound. *F Three*_____

2   The car security system works when somebody moves the car._____

3   The ExitGuard works when somebody touches the door._____

4   If there is a fire in a store, people can break open the ExitGuard._____

5   The burglar alarm works only on the windows._____

6   If the electrical circuit is broken, the burglar alarm will sound._____

3 Rotors and turbines

1 Look at the pictures and complete the crossword with words for labels 1–9. Use the words in column 3 of the Word list on the next page to help you.

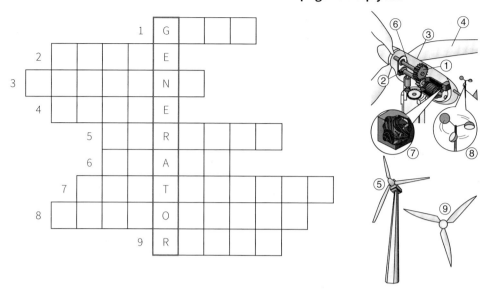

Crossword (down word: GENERATOR)

1 | G
2 | E
3 | N
4 | E
5 | R
6 | A
7 | T
8 | O
9 | R

2 ◀)) 11.1 Write the ten words from Exercise 1 next to their explanations. Then listen and repeat.

1 this produces electricity from the wind _turbine_

2 this measures the speed of the wind _____

3 this switches the wind turbine on and off _____

4 this slows down the rotating shaft _____

5 two of these make the high-speed shaft rotate at 1200 rpm
_____

6 the wind blows on the three _____

7 this produces electricity _____

8 this transmits rotation to the generator _____

9 this is a strong rigid container _____

10 this consists of three blades and a hub _____

3 ◀)) 11.2 Listen to the interview with a technician at a wind farm (a group of wind turbines). Circle the correct information.

1 In which state did the company open its first wind farm?
   a) New Mexico   b) Texas   c) California

2 When did the first part of the wind farm open?
   a) 2005   b) 2006   c) 2007

3 How many wind turbines are there on this wind farm?
   a) 102   b) 426   c) 626

4 How much of its electricity does Texas get from wind today?
   a) 10%   b) 20%   c) 30%

5 How many wind farms does the company have?
   a) 38   b) 48   c) 58

4 Word list

PISTONS & VALVES	SWITCHES & RELAYS	ROTORS & TURBINES	OTHER
NOUNS	**NOUNS**	**NOUNS**	**ADJECTIVES**
guard	armature	anemometer	electronic
high pressure	bell	blade	passive infrared
low pressure	burglar	brake	powerful
inlet valve	circuit	controller	**ADVERBS**
outlet valve	conductor	data	automatically
overflow pipe	contact	gear	wirelessly
piston	earth	generator	**VERBS**
piston pump	electromagnet	high-speed shaft	click
shaft	magnet	housing	detect
spring	metal core	hub	download
trigger	pivot	low-speed shaft	**NOUNS (noises)**
VERBS	relay switch	rotor	alarm bell
allow	sensor	tower	beep
cause	signal	wind turbine	buzzer
contract	speaker	**VERBS**	click
decrease	strip	blow	dial tone
expand	switch	contain	door bell
explode	transistor	transmit	horn
flow	wire		siren
force	wireless transmitter		
increase	**VERBS**		
let	sound		
prevent			
pump			
spread			

1 **Find opposites for these words in the Word list.**

1 allow _____ 4 suck _____

2 contract _____ 5 receive _____

3 increase _____ 6 inlet _____

2 **Find noises for these things in the NOUNS (noises) list in the Word list.**

1 the ___*beep*___ of an answerphone 5 the _____ of a telephone

2 the _____ of a car 6 the _____ of a police car

3 the _____ for a fire 7 the _____ on a door

4 the _____ of a mouse (2 choices)

1 Data

1 Circle the names of 11 words from the text on Course Book page 90. Some words are plurals. They go vertically from top to bottom, and sideways from left to right. No words go diagonally.

T	S	P	E	E	D	E	B	I	R	O	B	O	T	D
O	U	D	J	D	L	M	O	T	O	R	S	U	H	K
O	S	F	M	B	O	D	Y	I	Z	D	L	C	E	G
L	P	W	A	I	X	A	N	T	E	N	N	A	S	M
S	E	B	S	U	S	P	E	N	S	I	O	N	W	A
I	N	S	T	R	U	M	E	N	T	S	Q	E	H	R
R	S	C	A	M	E	R	A	S	W	K	L	R	Z	S

2 Read about the underwater robot Jason. Cross out the incorrect words.

JASON

Jason is a remotely operated vehicle (ROV). It weighs, (1) *in / on* the surface, a little (2) *over / near* 4000 kg. It can operate (3) *in / at* a maximum depth of 6500 metres. There are some cameras and lights mounted (4) *on / over* its body. When it is (5) *about / near* the sea bed, the cameras look (6) *around / over*.

Jason has two robot arms attached (7) *on / to* the front of its frame. There are special tools (8) *from / at* the end of each robot arm. Some of the tools collect water samples. Others collect rocks (9) *over / from* the sea floor. A small pump sucks (10) *on / in* living things. An instrument measures the temperature of the water. The first Jason started work in 1988 and worked (11) *up to / over* 2001. The new Jason 2 has made 1200 dives. It has spent (12) *near / at least* 16,000 hours at the bottom of the sea.

3 Write questions for these answers about Jason. Use the information in Exercise 2 and the verbs in brackets.

1 **Q:** What is *the underwater robot called* (call)?
  A: It's called Jason.

2 **Q:** How much _____ (weigh)?
  A: A little over 4000 kilos.

3 **Q:** Where _____ (be)?
  A: They're attached to the front of the frame.

4 **Q:** How _____ (collect)?
  A: A small pump sucks them in.

5 **Q:** Where _____ (be)?
  A: They're at the end of each robot arm.

6 **Q:** How many _____ (make)?
  A: At least 1200.

1 **A controller is training a mobile crane driver. Match the phrases in the two boxes.**

1 Press	a) the 'Start' button.
2 Press	b) forwards.
3 Release	c) to the left.
4 Push the joystick	d) the power switch.
5 Turn the wheel	e) the hand-brake.
6 Move forwards	f) 45° to the left.
7 Press	g) about 50 metres.
8 Rotate the arm	h) backwards.
9 Pull the joystick	i) backwards 10 metres.
10 Reverse	j) the brake pedal.

2 **Make sentences with verbs and phrases from the box.**

flies   goes   up and down   forwards and backwards
into space   over rocks and holes

1   A car _____ *goes forwards and backwards* _____ .

2   A helicopter _____ _____ .

3   A motorboat _____ _____ .

4   A plane _____ _____ .

5   A rover _____ _____ .

6   A space rocket _____ _____ .

7   A truck _____ _____ .

3 **Read again paragraph 1 of the text in Exercise 2 on page 58. The ship's crane is now lifting Jason from the sea floor. Put the verbs in brackets into the present continuous.**

A: Now, lift Jason up to the surface. Pull in the wire.

B: It (1) ___ *isn't moving* ___ (not move). Jason (2) _____ (not come) up. I think it's stuck to some rocks.

A: Move the arm of the crane to the left. Now raise the arm of the crane.

B: I (3) _____ (bring) it up.

A: What (4) _____ (happen) now? (5) _____ (the craft / move)?

B: Not yet. It's stuck.

A: Move the arm to the right. Bring the arm up fast and pull in the wire.

B: I (6) _____ (pull) it in now. Oh no!

A: What (7) _____ (happen)?

B: The wire (8) _____ (come) in very fast now. I think the wire is broken. And Jason (9) _____ (sit) on the sea bed.

1a Read the first half of the instructions for replacing a valve (1–5). Rewrite each instruction using the opposite verbs in the box.

assemble   attach   connect   loosen   take   tighten

1   Bring the large wrench from the workshop.
   Take the large wrench to the workshop.   `10`

2   Loosen the nuts on the supply pump.
   _____   ☐

3   Remove the pump from the supply pipe.
   _____   ☐

4   Dismantle the water pump.
   _____   ☐

5   Disconnect the valve from the pump.
   _____   ☐

1b 🔊 12.1 Number your answers in the correct order 6–10 to complete the instructions. Then listen, check and repeat.

2 🔊 12.2 The manager of an F1 racing team is talking to the engineer. Mark the jobs on the chart with a tick (✓) or a cross (✗). Write the days/dates for finishing the jobs.

Task	Y/N?	Date for finishing
1 Remove nose cone.	✓	*17 May*
2 Take photo of nose cone.		
3 Inspect fuel tank.		
4 Replace fuel pipe.		
5 Attach cables to foot pedals.		
6 Install new valves.		
7 Lubricate the gears.		
8 Test the car.		

3 Check your answers for 2 in the Answer key. Correct them if necessary. Write sentences about jobs 1–6 below.

1   (they) *They've removed the nose cone.*
2   (he) *He hasn't* _____. *He'll* _____
3   (they) _____
4   (they) _____
5   (he) _____
6   (he) _____

4 Word list

NOUNS		VERBS	VERBS
astronaut	oxygen	assemble	remain
camera	photograph	check	remove
control centre	progress	collect	replace
diameter	range	confirm	respond
equipment	robot	convert	roll
helicopter	robot arm	dismantle	support
instrument	rotation	include	train
laser	rover	inspect	**ADJECTIVES**
laser gun	simulation	install	controlled
mass	surface	lubricate	mobile
mast	suspension	operate	scientific
microphone	system	orbit	**ADVERBS**
million	titanium	prepare	approximately
obstacle	ventilation	range	over
	waste		less than
	weather station		more than
			under

1 **Find opposites in the Word list. Write them here.**

1 assemble _____

2 install _____

3 leave _____

4 exclude _____

5 more than _____

6 over _____

2 **Combine two nouns, one from each box, to make compound nouns. Write them below.**

laser	range
robot	system
six-wheel	tank
science	beam
suspension	arm
temperature	drive
waste	laboratory

laser beam, _____

_____

_____

Review Unit F

Section 1

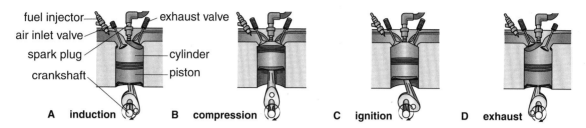

A induction B compression C ignition D exhaust

1 **Read about the four-stroke petrol engine shown in the pictures (A–D). Correct the sentences, using the verbs in brackets.**

A   The inlet valve opens. The round metal piston moves downwards. It stops the pressure inside the cylinder from falling.

(1)   *It makes the pressure inside the cylinder fall.* _____ (make)

This prevents a mixture of petrol and air from entering the cylinder.

(2)   _____ (allow)

B   The inlet valve closes. This lets the fuel mixture escape.

(3)   _____ (stop)

The piston moves upwards. This prevents the pressure in the cylinder from rising.

(4)   _____ (make)

C   The spark plug lights the fuel and doesn't allow it to explode.

(5)   _____ (cause)

This forces the piston downwards on its power stroke.

D   The outlet valve opens. The piston moves upwards. This stops the burnt fuel from escaping.

(6)   _____ (let)

2 **Complete the description of an electricity generating station in France. Use words from the box.**

blades   cables   ~~dam~~   electricity   gates   generator   shaft   turbine

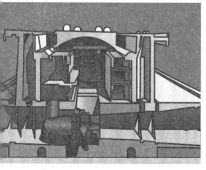

The (1) _____dam_____ across the River Rance in France was finished in 1966. Water flows from the river into the sea through the (2) _____ in the dam. Later, it flows back into the river from the sea. The water flows past the (3) _____ of a (4) _____ and makes it rotate. A (5) _____ connects the turbine to a (6) _____. The rotation of the generator produces (7) _____. The electricity leaves the power station through high-voltage (8) _____.

1 Write sentences about NASA's Mars rover Perseverance. Use the information from the specifications chart. Change the abbreviations to words.

1 Height	2.2 m	5 Wheels	aluminium and titanium
2 Length	3 m	6 Wheel diameter	52.5 cm
3 Weight	1025 kg	7 Max speed	152 metres per hour
4 Drive	6-wheel	8 Max/Min temperature range	−40 °C to +40 °C

1 _____*The rover is 2.2 metres high.*_____

2 _____*It has*_____.

3 _____

4 _____

5 _____

6 _____

7 _____

8 _____

2 Look at the progress chart for servicing a rover on 4 May. Complete the dialogue.

Task	Yes/No?	Date for finishing
1 Analyse rock samples	Y	4 May
2 Repair solar panel	N	tomorrow
3 Connect cables to solar panels	N	tomorrow
4 Replace damaged mast	Y	2 May
5 Assemble new robot arm	Y	1 May
6 Replace bent wheel	N	in progress
7 Service the brake system	N	7 May

A: Now, it's the 4th of May today. (1) _____*Have you analysed*_____ the rock samples?

B: Yes. We (2) _____*analysed*_____ them today.

A: Right. What about the solar panel? (3) _____*Have you repaired it yet?*_____

B: No, we (4) _____. We'll (5) _____ tomorrow.

A: Have you (6) _____ the cables to the solar panels?

B: No, not yet. (7) _____ tomorrow.

A: Right. What about the damaged mast? Have (8) _____?

B: Yes, we have. We (9) _____ the 2nd of May.

A: Right. What about the new robot arm? (10) _____?

B: Yes, we (11) _____ the 1st of May.

A: Have you (12) _____ the bent wheel yet?

B: No, we're still (13) _____ that.

A: What about the brake system? (14) _____?

B: No, we haven't. We (15) _____ the 7th of May.

Audio script

Unit 1 Check-up

🔊 1.1

I'm Alex Greyson, that's G–R–E–Y–S–O–N.
My phone number is 00 44 01962 804927.
My email address is alexg40@rossi.co.uk, that's A–L–E–X–G forty at rossi dot co dot uk.

🔊 1.2

Receptionist:	Welcome, Madam. Could you give me your surname, please?
Guest:	Yes, it's Johnstone. J–O–H–N–S–T–O–N–E.
Receptionist:	And your first name, Madam?
Guest:	Anne, with an E. So that's A–double N–E.
Receptionist:	And your company name, Madam?
Guest:	It's Weyco.
Receptionist:	How do you spell that?
Guest:	W–E–Y–C–O.
Receptionist:	Thank you. And your email address?
Guest:	It's aj309 at plas.com. That's A–J–three–oh–nine at plas.com. That's P–L–A–S dot com.
Receptionist:	Thank you. I've got that.

🔊 1.3

Mr Martin:	Has this car done a lot of kilometres?
Salesman:	It has done, er . . . 120 000 kilometres.
Mr Martin:	One hundred and twenty thousand! Oh! That's a lot.
Salesman:	It's a very nice car. I'll open the door for you. There!
Mr Martin:	Mmm. What's that inside the car?
Salesman:	That shows the temperature in the engine. Normally, it's 90° Celsius.
Mr Martin:	What's that on the right?
Salesman:	That's for the petrol tank.
Mr Martin:	How big is the tank?
Salesman:	It holds 55 litres.
Mr Martin:	That's good.
Salesman:	And the engine goes up to 6000 rpm.
Mr Martin:	Six thousand rpm? That's fast.
Salesman:	Yes. It can go at 185 kilometres per hour.
Mr Martin:	One hundred and eighty-five! Now that is fast! How much is it?
Salesman:	The price is 15 950 euros.
Mr Martin:	Is that all? Then I'll buy it!

Unit 2 Parts (1)

🔊 2.1

Message 1:	My name is Vladyslaw, that's V–L–A–D–Y–S–L–A–W Szczecin, that's spelt S–Z–C–Z–E–C–I–N. And my phone number is 00 48 920 4916.
Message 2:	My name is Abdel, that's A–B–D–E–L, Mohammed, that's M–O–H–A–double M–E–D, Mabrouk, that's M–A–B–R–O–U–K. My phone number is 00 20 537 1498.

🔊 2.2

Message 1:	Hello, I'm calling on the 14th of February and it's 11.45 now. Could you call me back, please? I need some parts for my car. My name is Jon, that's J–O–N, Bradleigh, that's B–R–A–D–L–E–I–G–H. And my phone number is 01962 4377. Thank you. Bye.
Message 2:	Hello, I'm calling at two thirty. The date today is er ehm the 30th of January. I need some parts for my car, so could you call me back, please? My name is Olof, that's O–L–O–F, Hansson, that's H–A–N–double S–O–N. My phone number is 01720 3399. Thanks.

🔊 2.3

Salesperson:	Hello. Customer Sales. Can I help you?
Customer:	Yes, I need some skateboard things.
Salesperson:	What do you need?
Customer:	I need some helmets.
Salesperson:	How many do you need?
Customer:	I need four large helmets.
Salesperson:	What colour?
Customer:	Red.
Salesperson:	So, that's four large red helmets.
Customer:	That's right. And I need to order some pads.
Salesperson:	How many do you need?
Customer:	I need six pads.
Salesperson:	Large, medium or small?
Customer:	Small, please.
Salesperson:	And what colour?
Customer:	Blue.
Salesperson:	So, that's six small blue pads. What's your name please?
Customer:	Webster, that's W–E–B–S–T–E–R.
Salesperson:	And your initials?
Customer:	My initial is S.
Salesperson:	And your address, please?
Customer:	14 Selly Park, that's two words, S–E–double L–Y, Park, that's P–A–R–K, Birmingham. That's B–I–R–M–I–N–G–H–A–M.

Salesperson:	And your postcode?
Customer:	BM29 8JE.
Salesperson:	And what's your phone number?
Customer:	0121 14 0433.
Salesperson:	OK, I've got that.

Unit 3 Parts (2)

◀) 3.1

Driver:	I have some boxes of speakers here. Where do you want them?
Manager:	Put them at the bottom, on the right.
Driver:	Where do the scanners go?
Manager:	They go . . . on the middle shelf, on the right.
Driver:	Where do you want the adapters?
Manager:	Adapters, er ehm, at the top, on the left.
Driver:	Mouse pads?
Manager:	What?
Driver:	Where do the mouse pads go?
Manager:	Mouse pads go on the bottom shelf, in the middle.
Driver:	Where do you want the printers?
Manager:	The printers go on the top shelf, on the right.
Driver:	Where do the headphones go?
Manager:	The headphones go on the top shelf, in the centre.
Driver:	Where do I put the amplifiers?
Manager:	Put those on the middle shelf, on the left.
Driver:	Flash drives? Where do they go?
Manager:	They go at the bottom, on the left.
Driver:	Keyboards? Where do you want those?
Manager:	Keyboards go . . . middle shelf, in the centre. Any more?
Driver:	No, that's all.

◀) 3.2

A:	There are lots of things here. Where do I put the multi-tool?
B:	Put the multi-tool above the hammer.
A:	Above the hammer. OK. Where do I put the pliers?
B:	Put those to the right of the dynamo.
A:	To the right of the dynamo. OK. Where does the radio go?
B:	The radio goes above the dynamo.
A:	OK. Where does the wrench go?
B:	The wrench goes . . . below the dynamo.
A:	Where do I put the batteries?
B:	Put those to the left of the flash drive.
A:	OK. Where do I put the torch?
B:	Put it to the right of the flash drive.
A:	To the right of the flash drive, so above the computer.
B:	That's good! Any more things?
A:	Yes, scissors.
B:	Put the scissors to the right of the wrench.
A:	That's all.

Unit 4 Movement

◀) 4.1

1   thirty kilometres per hour
2   five hundred revolutions per minute
3   fifteen metres per second
4   sixty-five miles per hour
5   eight kilometres per second

◀) 4.2

1   Sound travels at 300 metres per second.
2   The engine of a Formula 1 car turns at about 19 000 revolutions per minute.
3   The NASA Mars rover Perseverance travels at 152 metres per hour.
4   A solar-powered car can travel at 83 miles per hour.
5   A person on skis can go downhill at 248 kilometres per hour.
6   A person on a snowboard can go downhill at 201 kilometres per hour.
7   The maximum speed of a passenger train in China is 431 kilometres per hour.
8   The fastest sailing ship sails at 86 kilometres per hour.
9   A Blackbird jet flies at 1979 miles per hour.

◀) 4.3

A:	This is a list of the things in the box.
B:	Good!
A:	So, what's in the box? I can tick the things off on this list.
B:	Here's the truck. Look! It's very nice.
A:	What else?
B:	One antenna.
A:	For the truck or the transmitter?
B:	One for the transmitter, and . . . here we are . . . one on the truck.
A:	Batteries?
B:	One nine-volt battery.
A:	Only one? We need two.
B:	There's only one in the box.
A:	Oh dear. Do you have the instruction manual?
B:	No, it's not in the box.
A:	Oh no! Where is the instruction manual? We need it!
B:	Ah! I can see it. It's in your hand!

Unit 5 Flow

◀) 5.1

1   If the river is high, and the workshop is open, the current flows from the generator into the workshop.
2   If the river is high, and the workshop is closed, the current flows from the generator into the batteries.
3   If the river is low, and the workshop is open, the current flows from the batteries into the workshop.
4   If the river is low, and the workshop is closed, the current does not flow.
5   If the batteries are full, the current does not flow from the generator into the batteries.
6   If the batteries are empty, the current does not flow from the batteries into the workshop.

◀) 5.2

Customer:	I need some things for a solar power system. First, I need some solar panels.
Shopkeeper:	How many do you need?
Customer:	I need four 60-watt panels.
Shopkeeper:	Right. Anything else?
Customer:	Yes, I need a controller.

Shopkeeper:	How many amps?
Customer:	One five-amp controller.
Shopkeeper:	Right.
Customer:	And I need some batteries.
Shopkeeper:	How many do you need?
Customer:	I need four 12-volt 100-ampere hour batteries.
Shopkeeper:	Can you say that again?
Customer:	Yes, four batteries, 12 volt, 100 ampere hours.
Shopkeeper:	Right, that's clear.
Customer:	And I need some lamps.
Shopkeeper:	How many?
Customer:	I need six 12-volt 8-watt lamps.
Shopkeeper:	Six or sixteen lamps?
Customer:	Six lamps, please. And I need some cable.
Shopkeeper:	How many metres of cable do you want?
Customer:	I need 12 metres.
Shopkeeper:	What size?
Customer:	Six millimetre, 53 amps.
Shopkeeper:	Right.

Unit 6 Materials

🔊 6.1

Sales clerk:	And what equipment do you want to order?
Customer:	I need a backpack.
Sales clerk:	How many backpacks do you want?
Customer:	Only one.
Sales clerk:	And do you have the product number?
Customer:	Yes, it's 19 forward slash 124.
Sales clerk:	One nine forward slash 124. Now, we do the backpack in orange, red, green or blue. Which colour do you want?
Customer:	Er, ehm, green, please.
Sales clerk:	Now, the backpack comes in four different sizes, extra-large, large, medium or small. Which size do you want?
Customer:	Large, please.
Sales clerk:	OK. Next the material. You can have it in nylon or polyester.
Customer:	Polyester, please. I don't want a nylon one.
Sales clerk:	And the price is . . . 125 dollars. Or do you want the price in euros?
Customer:	No, dollars is fine. So, that's 125 dollars, then.

🔊 6.2

1 **A:** John. Can you give me your email address again, please?
B: OK. It's J Clarke with an E, so that's J–C–L–A–R–K–E, at i-way, that's I hyphen W–A–Y dot co dot U–K.
A: Can I check that? J–C–L–A–R–K–E, at i-way, that's I hyphen W–A–Y dot co dot U–K.
B: Correct.
2 **A:** Alex. Can I check your email address?
B: My email address is now Alex 2, that's A–L–E–X then number 2, at anti dash G–M dot org.
A: Org?
B: O–R–G.
A: Can I read it back to you? Alex 2, that's A–L–E–X then number 2, at anti dash G–M dot org.
B: That's right.

3 **A:** Sandrine, can I check your email address?
B: Yes. It's S underscore Hagen, that's H–A–G–E–N, at Rhyno dot FR.
A: How do you spell 'Rhyno'?
B: R–H–Y–N–O.
A: So that's S underscore Hagen, that's H–A–G–E–N, at Rhyno dot F–R. F–R not F–R–A?
B: Yes. That's right.

🔊 6.3

1 **A:** Here's a good website for news.
B: OK. What is it?
A: C–C dot co forward slash newsline.
B: Is newsline one word?
A: Yes. N–E–W–S–L–I–N–E.
2 **A:** Do you know a good website for live radio?
B: Yes. Try this one. It's live dash raydio – that's R–A–Y–D–I–O – dot net.
A: Live dash raydio dot net. Thanks.
3 **A:** Do you know the website for the toy company?
B: Yes. It's rc toyz, that's R–C toyz dot com forward slash 51.
A: Is rc toys R–C–T–O–Y–S?
B: No, it's R–C–T–O–Y–Z.
A: So that's rc toyz dot com forward slash 51.
B: Correct.

Unit 7 Specifications

🔊 7.1

Shopkeeper:	Hello. Can I help you?
Customer:	Yes, I'm repairing my workshop and I'm looking at your order form. First, I need some paint.
Shopkeeper:	How much paint do you need?
Customer:	Oh, about 40 litres.
Shopkeeper:	What colour paint do you need?
Customer:	Green.
Shopkeeper:	And what size tin do you need? We have five-litre tins and ten-litre tins.
Customer:	I need four ten-litre tins, please.
Shopkeeper:	Four ten-litre tins. Do you have the product number on the order form?
Customer:	Yes, it's P 176 G–R.
Shopkeeper:	OK. Anything else?
Customer:	I need some cement.
Shopkeeper:	How much cement do you need? We sell it in 10-kilo bags and 20-kilo bags. How many bags do you need?
Customer:	I need five 20-kilo bags, please.
Shopkeeper:	Five 20-kilo bags. What colour? White or grey?
Customer:	White, please.
Shopkeeper:	What's the product number, please?
Customer:	It's C zero one one six W.
Shopkeeper:	OK.
Customer:	Now, do you have any screws?
Shopkeeper:	Yes. What size do you need?
Customer:	24 mil.
Shopkeeper:	How many screws do you need?
Customer:	About four hundred.

Shopkeeper:	We sell them in packets of 50 or 100.
Customer:	So I need four packets of one hundred.
Shopkeeper:	And the product number, please?
Customer:	S 00941.
Shopkeeper:	OK. Do you need any nails?
Customer:	No. I don't need any nails, thanks.

🔊 7.2

1. How much paint do you need?
2. What colour paint do you need?
3. What size tin do you need?
4. How much cement do you need?
5. How many bags do you need?
6. Do you have any screws?
7. How many screws do you need?
8. Do you need any nails?

Unit 8 Reporting

🔊 8.1

1. They have bent the router antenna.
2. The user manual is torn.
3. Someone has broken the camera.
4. The body of the radio is cracked.
5. The speakers are damaged.
6. Someone has cut the power cable.
7. The lenses of the goggles are scratched.
8. I have burnt my overalls.
9. They have dented the car door.

🔊 8.2

Part 1

Helpdesk:	Helpdesk. Please can I have your order number?
Customer:	Yes, it's PC zero eight. Forward slash one zero two zero. Forward slash double zero one seven.
Helpdesk:	OK. I've got that. Can I check your details? You're Mr Bert Sandle?
Customer:	Yes, but you spelt my name wrong. It's B–U–R–T and then S–A–N–D–E double L.
Helpdesk:	B–U–R–T, S–A–N–D–E double L. I'm sorry about that. And can I check your address, Mr Sandell? Is it 14 Hayford Road, Catford, London?
Customer:	Yes, but you've got the wrong postcode. My postcode is S–E ten, four Q–Y.
Helpdesk:	S–E ten, four Q–Y. And your telephone number?
Customer:	0208 4114009.
Helpdesk:	Good, I've got that. And your email address?
Customer:	It's bsandell87@pdq.com.
Helpdesk:	Can you repeat that, please?
Customer:	Yes, it's B–S–A–N–D–E double L eight seven at P–D–Q dot com.
Helpdesk:	At P–D–Q dot com. OK, I've got that.

🔊 8.3

Part 2

Helpdesk:	Now, you bought a computer from us. How can I help you?
Customer:	I think somebody dropped the box. Some things are damaged and some things are missing.
Helpdesk:	Oh, I'm sorry to hear that. What's missing?
Customer:	The mouse is missing.
Helpdesk:	Mouse missing. Anything else?
Customer:	You know the antenna on the router? Well, it's bent.
Helpdesk:	Antenna bent. Is there any more damage?
Customer:	Yes, the computer screen is scratched.
Helpdesk:	OK. Computer screen scratched.
Customer:	And the keyboard is broken.
Helpdesk:	Broken?
Customer:	Yes, it's broken.
Helpdesk:	Keyboard broken. Anything else?
Customer:	There's no plug on the power cable.
Helpdesk:	No plug on cable. Is that all?
Customer:	There's some more damage: the left-hand speaker is damaged.
Helpdesk:	Left-hand speaker damaged.
Customer:	And the right-hand speaker has a hole in the front.
Helpdesk:	Hole in the front of right-hand speaker. Is that all?
Customer:	The user manual is missing.
Helpdesk:	No user manual.
Customer:	That's all.
Helpdesk:	Oh dear. I'm very sorry about this. Please put everything back in the box. We'll collect it from your house and we'll bring you a new computer.
Customer:	That's good.
Helpdesk:	Thank you for calling, Mr Sandell.

Unit 9 Troubleshooting

🔊 9.1

Dialogue 1

Technician:	Hello. How can I help you?
Customer 1:	My computer isn't working.
Technician:	OK. Is it plugged in?
Customer 1:	Yes, it is.
Technician:	And is the adapter connected to a power source?
Customer 1:	Ah! No, it isn't. I'll connect it now. Right. I've connected it, but it still isn't working.
Technician:	OK. And is the power switch up or down?
Customer 1:	It was up, but now I've switched it down. Ah! It's working now!

Dialogue 2

Technician:	Hello. How can I help you?
Customer 2:	My smart speaker isn't working.
Technician:	I see. Is your laptop working?
Customer 2:	Yes, it's working and the battery is fully charged.
Technician:	Is the adapter for the speaker connected to a power source?
Customer 2:	Yes, it is.
Technician:	Is the power switch up or down?
Customer 2:	It's down.
Technician:	Is the speaker connected to the adapter?
Customer 2:	No, it isn't connected. It's come out. I'm sorry. I'll connect it now.

Dialogue 3

Technician: Hello. What can I do for you?

Customer 3: I have a problem with my computer. I've switched it on, but it doesn't work properly.

Technician: Is the display on or off?

Customer 3: It's on, but the mouse isn't working.

Technician: Does your computer mouse have a cord or is it wireless?

Customer 3: It's a Wi-Fi mouse, I think.

Technician: OK. And how long have you had your computer?

Customer 3: About five months.

Technician: Did you charge the battery in your mouse after you bought it?

Customer 3: No, I didn't.

Technician: Aha. I think I've found the problem. The battery in your mouse isn't charged.

🔊 9.2

Dialogue 1

Technician: Does the computer start?

Customer: No, it doesn't.

Technician: Right. Press the power button again.

Dialogue 2

Technician: Is the power switch down?

Customer: No, it isn't.

Technician: OK. Press it down.

Dialogue 3

Technician: Are the loudspeakers connected?

Customer: No, they aren't.

Technician: OK. Connect them.

Dialogue 4

Technician: Is the adapter connected?

Customer: Yes, it is.

Technician: Good.

Dialogue 5

Technician: Do the loudspeakers work?

Customer: No, they don't.

Technician: OK. Connect them and try again.

Dialogue 6

Technician: Are the two LED lights on?

Customer: Yes, they are.

Technician: Good.

Dialogue 7

Technician: Does the computer start?

Customer: Yes, it does.

Technician: Good.

Dialogue 8

Technician: Do the loudspeakers work now?

Customer: Yes, they do.

Technician: Good.

Unit 10 Safety

🔊 10.1

Worker: There's been an accident!

Supervisor: Oh no! Was anybody hurt?

Worker: Yes, Peter, the storeman.

Supervisor: Where is he now?

Worker: He's gone to hospital.

Supervisor: OK. I must fill in this form. First, where did the accident happen?

Worker: In Number 6 workshop.

Supervisor: In Number 6 workshop. And when did it take place?

Worker: At half-past three this afternoon.

Supervisor: So, 3.30 pm. And today is . . .

Worker: The twenty-ninth of March

Supervisor: Thanks. So, what's the name of the injured person?

Worker: Peter Graski. That's G–R–A–S–K–I.

Supervisor: OK. What does he do? What's his job?

Worker: He's the storeman.

Supervisor: S–T–O–R–E–M–A–N. Did he injure anybody else?

Worker: No, only himself.

Supervisor: So nobody else. What exactly happened?

Worker: He lifted a bar of steel alone. And he hurt his back. So he dropped the bar on his boot. His foot is injured.

Supervisor: So, he didn't slip and he didn't trip and he didn't fall, but he lifted something and he dropped something. And you say his back is injured.

Worker: Yes, his back and his foot.

Supervisor: And you say he's not at work now.

Worker: Correct. He's gone to hospital.

🔊 10.2

1 First, where did the accident happen?
2 Was anybody hurt?
3 When did it take place?
4 What's the name of the injured person?
5 What does he do?
6 What's his job?
7 Did he injure anybody else?
8 What happened?

Unit 11 Cause and Effect

🔊 11.1

1 turbine
2 anemometer
3 controller
4 brake
5 gear
6 blades
7 generator
8 shaft
9 housing
10 rotor

Interviewer:	In which state did you open your first wind farm? Was that in California?
Technician:	No. It was right here in Texas.
Interviewer:	And when was that?
Technician:	The first part opened in 2005. The second part opened in 2006. And the third part in 2007.
Interviewer:	I see. How many wind turbines are there on this wind farm?
Technician:	Let me see. Four hundred twenty-six, plus two hundred. That makes six hundred twenty-six.
Interviewer:	So many wind turbines! How much of the electricity that you generate in Texas comes from wind?
Interviewer:	It used to be about 10 percent. But now it's over 20 percent.
Interviewer:	Really?
Technician:	And some states in the USA get over 30, 40 or 50 percent of their electricity from wind.
Interviewer:	Do you have any other wind farms?
Technician:	Of course. We have wind farms in many states of the USA. Right now, we have a total of 48 wind farms.
Interviewer:	That must add up to a lot of wind turbines!
Technician:	You're right! And they make a lot of electricity for our customers.

Unit 12 Checking and confirming

1   Bring the large wrench from the workshop.
2   Loosen the nuts on the supply pump.
3   Remove the pump from the supply pipe.
4   Dismantle the water pump.
5   Disconnect the valve from the pump.
    Replace the valve.
6   Connect the valve to the pump.
7   Assemble the water pump.
8   Attach the pump to the supply pipe.
9   Tighten the nuts on the supply pipe.
10 Take the large wrench to the workshop.

Manager:	Hello. I'm checking progress on the repairs to our Formula 1 car.
Engineer:	One moment. I'll get the progress chart. OK.
Manager:	It's the 17th of May today. Have you removed the damaged nose cone yet?
Engineer:	Yes, we have.
Manager:	Good. So I can put a tick against that job. And have you taken a photo of the nose cone?
Engineer:	No, not yet.
Manager:	When will you do that?
Engineer:	I'll do it today, the 17th of May.
Manager:	OK. Now, the next thing on my list. Have you inspected the fuel tank yet?
Engineer:	Yes, we have. It was damaged.
Manager:	So, you haven't replaced the fuel pipe yet.
Engineer:	Correct. We haven't.
Manager:	When will you do that job?
Engineer:	We'll do that on the 19th of May.
Manager:	The 19th of May. OK. Now, the next thing on my list. Have you attached the cables to the foot pedals?
Engineer:	Yes, I've finished that job.
Manager:	And have you installed the new valves on the engine yet?
Engineer:	Yes, I've done that too.
Manager:	Now. Lubricating the gears. Have you done that job yet?
Engineer:	No. We'll do that on the 20th of May.
Manager:	And you need to test the car. When will you do that?
Engineer:	If everything is OK, we'll test the car on the 22nd of May.
Manager:	Good! I've noted all that information. Thanks.

Answer key

1 Check-up

1 Basics

1
1 I'm, is
2 Where, What
3 Are, I'm, What's

2
1 Stand up.
2 Write your name.
3 Turn right.
4 Close your book.
5 Sit down.
6 Raise your hand.
7 Come in.

3

Tools	Electricals	Fixings
chisel	adapter	bolts
saw	antenna	nuts
screwdriver	cable	screws
spanner	plug	washers

2 Letters and numbers

1
Rossi Air
Alex Gr**e**yson
Aerospace Technician
Tel: + 44 (0)19**6**2 80**4**927
Email: alexg**40**@rossi**.co.uk**

2
Surname: Johnstone
First name: Anne
Company: Weyco
Email address: aj309@plas.com

3
1 gallon
2 euro
3 kilogram
4 amp/ampere
5 inch
6 foot
7 kilometre
8 angle/degree
9 gram
10 Celsius
11 positive
12 metre
13 kilowatt
14 volt
15 kilometres per hour
16 revolutions per minute
17 watt
18 litre
19 pound
20 negative

4
1 Kilometres: 120 000 km
2 Engine temperature: 90° Celsius
3 Petrol tank: 55 litres
4 Engine speed: up to 6000 rpm
5 Top speed: 185 kph
6 Price: 15 950 euros

3 Dates and times

1
4th	fourth	5th	fifth
12th	twelfth	29th	twenty-ninth
23rd	twenty-third	8th	eighth
7th	seventh	31st	thirty-first
30th	thirtieth	6th	sixth
22nd	twenty-second	20th	twentieth

2
1 The thirty-first of January is a Friday, so the eighth of February is a Saturday.
2 The twenty-ninth of March is a Wednesday, so the second of April is a Sunday.
3 The twenty-ninth of May is a Tuesday, so the third of June is a Sunday.
4 The thirtieth of July is a Thursday, so the fourth of August is a Tuesday.
5 The twenty-eighth of September is a Monday, so the seventh of October is a Wednesday.
6 The twenty-seventh of November is a Thursday, so the sixth of December is a Saturday.

3
A: When's the meeting?
B: It's on Monday.
A: Is that Monday the 12th?
B: Yes. That's right.
A: Do you know what time?
B: It's at 10 o'clock.
A: OK. See you then. Bye.
B: Bye.

4
1 five thirty
2 two fifteen in the
3 It's seven fifty-five in the
4 It's eleven forty

4 Word list

Sample answers

1 425 grams   22 kilograms
2 23° Celsius
3 23 metres   6 foot/feet   12 inches
4 79 kilometres
5 110 kilometres per hour
6 3500 revolutions per minute
7 45 litres
8 6000 euros
9 Two hundred and twenty-five volts

2 Parts (1)

1 Naming

1
1 That's the wheel of a racing car.
2 That's the axle of a mountain bike.
3 That's the nose of a plane.
4 That's the number plate of a motorbike.
5 That's the tail of a rocket.
6 That's the deck of a boat.

2
1 That isn't a hammer. That's a screwdriver.
2 Those aren't screws. Those are nails.
3 This isn't a chisel. This is a spanner.
4 These aren't washers. These are nuts.
5 This isn't a nail. This is a staple.
6 These aren't nuts. These are bolts.
7 That isn't a staple. That's a screw.
8 Those aren't nuts. Those are washers.

2 Assembling

1 1 Raise the car with the jack.
2 Loosen all the nuts with the box spanner.
3 Take off all the nuts.
4 Take the wheel off the axle.
5 Put the spare wheel on the axle.
6 Put on all the nuts.
7 Tighten all the nuts with the box spanner.
8 Lower the car.

2 Shopkeeper: Hello.
Customer: Hello. I need some nails, please.
Shopkeeper: Some nails. What size do you need?
Customer: 30 mil, please.
Shopkeeper: 30 mil. How many nails do you need?
Customer: I need 80, please.

3 Ordering

1 1 Name: Vlad**y**slaw S**zczec**in
Phone number: 00 48 920 4**9**16

2 Name: Abdel Moha**mm**ed Mab**rou**k
Phone number: 00 20 537 149**8**

2

1	2
Date: 14 February	Date: 30 January
Time: 11.45	Time: 2.30
Caller: Jon Bradleigh	Caller: Olof Hansson
Phone number:	Phone number:
01962 4377	01720 3399

3 Surname: Webster, S
Address: 14 Selly Park, Birmingham
Postal code: BM29 8JE
Tel: 0121 14 0433
Order: four large red helmets, six small blue pads, no decks

4 Word list

1 wheel, hammer, spanner, assemble, loosen, pull, small, yellow

2 Tools: hammer, lever, screwdriver, spanner
Other things: bolt, nail, nut, screw, staple, washer

3 Before skateboarding
Put on the helmet.
Push it down onto your head.
Tighten the helmet strap.
Put on the pads.
Tighten the pads.

After skateboarding
Loosen the pads and take them off.
Loosen the helmet strap and take off the helmet.

REVIEW UNIT A

Section 1

1 1 Are, I'm, That's   2 do, I'm
3 Is, he's

2 1 1 February 2021   4 12 November 2021
2 9 March 2021   5 8 July 2021
3 22 January 2021   6 9 October 2021

3 1 Monday, the first of May
2 Thursday, the fourth of May
3 Sunday, the seventh of May
4 Wednesday, the tenth of May
5 Saturday, the thirteenth of May
6 Tuesday, the sixteenth of May
7 Friday, the nineteenth of May
8 Monday, the twenty-second of May

Section 2

1 1 bolts   4 nuts   7 skateboards
2 washers   5 nails
3 screws   6 axles

2 A: What's this tool called?
B: It's a hammer.
A: Is it for screws?
B: No. It's for nails.

3 A: Hello. I need to order some business cards.
B: How many do you need?
A: 200, please.
B: What size cards do you need?
A: 85 millimetres by 55 millimetres.
B: What's your name?
A: Stevens, with a V. Initials HC.
B: What's your address and postal code?
A: 14 Hayfield Road, Bristol BR7 4JK.
B: What's your phone number?
A: 0117 893462.
B: What's your email address?
A: It's harry.stevens@ojs.com.
B: When do you want them?
A: Friday, please.

3 Parts (2)

1 Tools

1 1 scissors   7 pliers
2 screw   8 chisel
3 ruler   9 cover
4 hammer   10 can opener
5 wrench   11 spanner
6 blade   Vertical word: screwdriver

2 1 screwdriver   4 spanner
2 hammer   5 pair of pliers
3 pair of scissors   6 saw

3 1 Does, doesn't, Does, does, have, has
2 Do, don't, Do, do, have, has

2 Functions

1a/b 1 generator   6 electricity
2 compass   7 temperature
3 battery   8 handle
4 adapter   9 thermometer
5 antenna   10 dynamo

2
1. turn
2. turns
3. charges
4. shine
5. listen
6. charge

3 Locations

1

8 adapters	5 headphones	9 printers
6 amplifiers	2 keyboards	4 scanners
3 flash drives	7 mouse pads	1 speakers

2

batteries 1	pliers 9
torch 3	wrench 11
radio 5	scissors 12
multi-tool 7	

4 Word list

1. Chisels cut wood into a shape.
2. Hammers drive in nails.
3. Pliers grip wire.
4. Rulers measure everything.
5. Saws cut wood or metal.
6. Scissors cut paper.
7. Screwdrivers loosen screws.
8. Wrenches tighten nuts.

4 Movement

1 Directions

1 A vertical take-off (Picture 4)
A short take-off (Picture 1)
vertically up (D), horizontal (B, C), diagonally up (A)

2
1. straight up
2. forwards
3. to the right
4. up and down
5. sideways
6. straight down

3
1. pivots
2. directions
3. ankle
4. degrees
5. move
6. rotate
7. hip
8. angles
9. knee
10. sideways

2 Instructions

1
1. thirty kilometres per hour
2. five hundred revolutions per minute
3. fifteen metres per second
4. sixty-five miles per hour
5. eight kilometres per second

2
1. 300 m/s
2. 19 000 rpm
3. 152 metres per hour
4. 83 mph
5. 248 kph
6. 201 kph
7. 431 kph
8. 86 kph
9. 1979 mph

3 Instruction manual (✔)
Transmitter (✔)
Truck (✔)
Antenna for transmitter (✔)
Antenna for truck (✔)
Two 9 V batteries (only one)

4
1. sends
2. receives
3. use
4. control
5. turns
6. Press
7. moves

3 Actions

1
1. G
2. F
3. B
4. A
5. C
6. D
7. E

2
1. When you pull the gear lever to 'R', the car reverses.
2. When you pull the gear lever to 'D', the car moves forwards.
3. When you press the accelerator, the car goes faster.
4. When you press the brake pedal a little, the car goes slower.
5. When you turn the steering wheel to the right, the car turns right.
6. When you turn the steering wheel to the left, the car turns left.
7. When you press the brake pedal, the car stops.

4 Word list

1 accelerator, antenna (for the radio), brake, handle (for a door), lever, parking brake, pedal, steering wheel, power switch (for the lights)

2 accelerate / slow down
ascend / descend
pull / push
forwards / backwards
up / down
to the left / to the right

3 Helicopters can accelerate, ascend, descend, reverse, rotate, slow down, turn round.

4
1. Drive forwards slowly. Stop.
2. Reverse and turn the steering wheel to the left.
3. Reverse a little more and turn the steering wheel to the right. Stop.
4. Drive forwards a little and turn the steering wheel to the left.

REVIEW UNIT B

Section 1

1
1. The screen is in the centre. (✔)
2. The keyboard is in the centre, <u>below</u> the screen.
3. The TV is to the <u>left</u> of the screen.
4. The printer is below the screen. (✔)
5. Speaker 1 is on the <u>left</u>.
6. Speaker 2 is on the <u>right</u>.
7. The mouse is at the <u>bottom</u>, to the <u>right</u> of the keyboard.
8. The headphones are to the <u>right</u> of the screen, above speaker 2.

2

football	planes	the news
bikes	science	cars
boats	skateboards	space

1   Football is at the top, on the left.
2   Planes are at the top, in the centre.
3   The news is at the top, on the right.
4   Bikes are on the middle line, on the left.
5   Science is on the middle line, in the centre.
6   Cars are on the middle line, on the right.
7   Boats are at the bottom, on the left.
8   Skateboards are at the bottom, in the centre.
9   Space is at the bottom, on the right.

3   1   battery, hammer, spanner, wrench
     2   a pair of overalls, a pair of pincers, a pair of pliers, a pair of scissors

Section 2

1a/b   1   D: forwards and backwards
       2   C: rotate
       3   A: descend, diagonal or horizontal
       4   B: up and down

2a/b   1   Can you find the user manual?
          No, I can't find it.
       2   How does the truck work?
          It receives signals from the transmitter.
       3   Where do I put the battery?
          You put it in the transmitter.
       4   Where does the antenna go?
          It goes on top of the truck.
       5   How do I steer the truck?
          You press one of the control buttons.
       6   Are there two batteries in the box?
          No, there is only one.
       7   Do we need a second battery?
          Yes, we need it for the truck.

3   1   Start the engine. Tie the rope on the <u>left</u> of the boat to Point x.
     2   Turn the steering wheel to the left. Push the engine lever forwards; this moves the boat slowly <u>forwards</u> and to the <u>left</u>.
     3   Pull the engine lever to the <u>middle</u> position. Loosen the rope. Take off the rope from Point X.
     4   Turn the steering wheel to the <u>middle</u> position. Pull the lever <u>backwards</u>; this puts the engine into reverse. Reverse slowly.

5 Flow

1 Heating system

1

sink / rise	out of / into	enter / leave
above / below	cold / hot	outlet / inlet
bottom / top	cool / heat	push / pull

2   1   A fridge cools water.
     2   Cold water sinks to the bottom of a water tank.
     3   The outlet pipe for hot water is above the pump.
     4   Water leaves the tank through the outlet pipe.
     5   Pull the shower head out of the pipe.

3   1   above   5   out of   9   leaves
     2   below   6   flows   10 to
     3   pushes   7   through
     4   into   8   rises

2 Electrical circuit

1   1   lamp   5   electrical current
     2   solar panel   6   controller
     3   battery   7   cable
     4   switch

2   1   If the river is high, and the workshop is open, the current flows from the generator into the workshop.
     2   If the river is high, and the workshop is closed, the current flows from the generator into the batteries.
     3   If the river is low, and the workshop is open, the current flows from the batteries into the workshop.
     4   If the river is low, and the workshop is closed, the current does not flow.
     5   If the batteries are full, the current does not flow from the generator into the batteries.
     6   If the batteries are empty, the current does not flow from the batteries into the workshop.

3   1c, 2b, 3b, 4c, 5b

3 Cooling system

1   1   minus two degrees Fahrenheit
     2   twenty-one degrees Celsius
     3   seventy-five degrees Fahrenheit
     4   minus eight degrees Celsius
     5   twenty-four degrees Celsius
     6   thirty-three degrees Celsius

2   1   The water pump   6   Cool water
     2   Two hoses   7   The fan
     3   The thermostat   8   Cool water
     4   Hot water   9   The engine
     5   The fan

3   1   From the spring, water flows to a reservoir at the top of the hill.
     2   From the reservoir, water passes through a pipe to the field.
     3   The pipe goes into a field of fruit trees.
     4   Water leaves the pipe through small holes.
     5   The water then flows around the fruit trees.
     6   A little water flows out of the bottom of the field.
     7   This water enters a tank at the bottom of the hill.

4 Word list

1   1   enters   3   heats   5   sinks
     2   flows   4   rises   6   leaves

2   1d, 2a, 3e, 4b, 5c

6 Materials

1 Materials testing

1
1. You can bend metal, but you can't bend wood.
2. You can heat air and you can heat water.
3. You can melt plastic, but you can't melt wood.
4. You can scratch glass and you can scratch metal.
5. You can stretch nylon, but you can't stretch glass.
6. You can break glass and you can break wood.
7. You can cut wood and you can cut metal.
8. You can compress air, but you can't compress glass.

2
1	are testing	5	is running
2	is sitting	6	is stretching
3	is tightening	7	is touching
4	is starting	8	Is the dummy's face striking

3
1. A: Are you pushing the handles?
   B: No, I'm rowing.
2. A: Is he walking?
   B: No, he's running.
3. A: Is she bending the wall bars?
   B: No, she's climbing the wall bars.
4. A: Are you pulling the bar down?
   B: No, I'm pushing the bar up.
5. A: Is she rotating her legs?
   B: No, she's stretching her legs.
6. A: Is he pushing the bar?
   B: No, he's picking the bar up.

2 Materials and their properties

1 Horizontal: plastic, composite, fibreglass, titanium, concrete, ceramic, graphite
Vertical: aluminium, steel, nylon, rubber, polystyrene, polycarbonate, diamond

2
1. A ceramic cup is heat-resistant and hard.
2. A concrete floor is rigid and tough.
3. A rubber tyre is flexible and strong.
4. A fibreglass window frame is heat-resistant and rigid.
5. A nylon rope is flexible and strong.
6. The graphite in the middle of a pencil is light and soft.
7. A polycarbonate road sign is rigid and strong.
8. A polystyrene coffee cup is brittle and light.

3
1. The nose cone is made of aluminium.
2. The wheels are made of aluminium alloy.
3. The tyres are made of rubber composite.
4. The frame is made of composite.
5. The inside is made of fibreglass.
6. The seats are made of plastic.
7. The engine is made of aluminium alloy.
8. The wings are made of aluminium alloy.

3 Buying

1 Product name: backpack
Product no: 19/124
Quantity: one
Colour: green
Size: large
Material: polyester
Price: $125

2
1. jclarke@i-way.co.uk
2. alex2@anti-gm.org
3. s_hagen@rhyno.fr

3
1. cc.co/newsline
2. live-raydio.net
3. rctoyz.com/51

4 *Sample answers*
1. What's your surname, please?
2. Could you spell that, please?
3. What's your phone number, please?
4. What's your email address, please?
5. Could you repeat that, please?
6. How many helmets do you need?
7. What colour would you like?
8. And how do you want to pay?

4 Word list

1
1. The nose cone is made of fibreglass.
2. The wheels are made of aluminium alloy.
3. The frame is made of cromoly, a steel alloy.
4. The tyres are made of rubber composite.
5. The radiator is made of aluminium.
6. The engine is made of aluminium alloy.
7. The pistons are coated with ceramic.
8. The wings are made of polystyrene and fibreglass.

2
1	strong	3	soft	5	light
2	brittle	4	flexible		

REVIEW UNIT C

Section 1

1
1	1	that	2 6	here
	2	here	7	This
	3	are	8	How
	4	thanks	9	about
	5	OK	10	I'm

2
1. bending, climbing, heating, holding, pulling, pushing
2. cutting, dropping, gripping, running, sitting, swimming
3. diving, driving, leaving, moving, rising, striking

3
A: Is everything OK?
B: No. The engine's cooling system isn't working. The temperature of the water is rising.
A: Is the fan blowing air through the radiator?
B: Yes, the fan is fine.
A: Is the pump pushing water round the engine?
B: Yes, the pump is working.
A: Look! That clip on the bottom hose is loose. Water is running out of the hose. So the cold water is not going back to the engine. Tighten the clip. Is the water running out of the hose now?
B: No.
A: Check the temperature.
B: Ah! The temperature is dropping. Good!

Section 2

1 If you warm ice cubes, they melt.
If you pull a rubber band, it stretches.
If you strike a ceramic cup very hard, it breaks.
If you heat water to 100 °Celsius, it boils.
If you pour cool water into a radiator, it sinks.
If you heat pieces of wood, they burn.

2

Part	Material	Properties
board	polystyrene, fibreglass	strong, light
mast	polycarbonate	strong, flexible
boom	aluminium, rubber	rigid, strong
sail	nylon, polyester	light, strong
rope	nylon	strong
daggerboard	polycarbonate	rigid
fin	polycarbonate	rigid
pivot	rubber	strong, flexible

7 Specifications

1 Dimensions

1 A: bridge, B: tunnel, C: road, D: cable, E: pylon,
F: pier, G: deck, H: span

2 1 The sea has a depth of 270 metres.
2 The river is 25 metres deep.
3 The span is 330 metres long.
4 The pylons have a height of 160 metres.
5 The length of the road is 22 kilometres.
6 The deck has a width of 8 metres.

3 1 Where is this bridge?
It's in China.
2 How long is the inner span?
It's 1490 metres.
3 How high are the pylons?
They're 215 metres high.
4 How wide is the deck?
It's 39.2 metres.
5 How high is the deck above the water?
It's 50 metres above the water.

2 Quantities

1 1 2003
2 40
3 metres
4 reinforced concrete
5 steel
6 aluminium
7 glass
8 area
9 square metres
10 18
11 metres per second
12 circle
13 small
14 wide

2

Item	Kind	Size	Product number	Quantity
Paint	green	10 litre tin	P176GR	4
Cement	white	20 kg bag	C0116W	5
Nails	packet of 50 / 100	24 / 30 mm	N420 / N240	None
Screws	packet of 100	24 mm	S00941	4

3 1 How much paint do you need?
2 What colour paint do you need?
3 What size tin do you need?
4 How much cement do you need?
5 How many bags do you need?
6 Do you have any screws?
7 How many screws do you need?
8 Do you need any nails?

3 Future projects

1

Brenner Base Tunnel (BBT)	
Location of tunnel	between Austria and Italy
Completion date	2032
Number of tunnels	2
Length of tunnels	55 kilometres
Height above sea level	794 metres
Maximum speed of trains	250 kph
Source of power for trains	electricity
Number of trains per day	400

2 1 They're building a new tunnel.
2 There'll be two new tunnels.
3 They'll finish the tunnel in 2032.
4 The trains won't use magnetism.
5 There'll be about 400 trains per day.

3 The BBT will be the second longest <u>railway</u> tunnel in the world. It will connect Italy and <u>Austria</u>. Engineers will finish the project in <u>2032</u>. The new tunnel will be about 790 metres <u>above</u> sea level. There will be about 400 trains per <u>day</u>. The new trains will use <u>electricity</u>. <u>Some</u> of them will run at 250 kph.

4 Word list

1 length, height, width, depth

2 a bottle of oil
a tube of glue / superglue
a bag of cement
a packet of screws
a tin of paint

3 1 lay the foundations
2 build the piers
3 put the pylons on the piers
4 attach the cables to the pylons
5 make the deck
6 fix the deck to the cables
7 lay the road

8 Reporting

1 Recent incidents

1 check, checked, checked
change, changed, changed
stop, stopped, stopped
cut, cut, cut
buy, bought, bought
sell, sold, sold
fall, fell, fallen
speak, spoke, spoken
take, took, taken

2 A: Have you spoken to Security?
B: Yes, I have.
A: Good. Have you rung the new customer?
B: No, I haven't. I'll do it now.
A: Have you sent an email to HTB?
B: Yes, I have.
A: Good. Have you written the incident report?
B: No, I haven't. I'll do it now.

3 1 Hello? Police? A thief has taken my digger.
2 Police? A man has driven a digger into the town centre here.
3 Hello? A digger has crashed into a shop window in Broad Street.
4 Help! Two men have come into my shop in Broad Street.
5 One man has broken the display case with a sledgehammer.
6 The two thieves have stolen some diamonds.
7 Two men with bags have run down to the river.
8 The two men have jumped into a motor boat. They are on the river now.

2 Damage and loss

1 1 They have bent the router antenna.
2 The user manual is torn.
3 Someone has broken the camera.
4 The body of the radio is cracked.
5 The speakers are damaged.
6 Someone has cut the power cable.
7 The lenses of the goggles are scratched.
8 I have burnt the overalls.
9 They have dented the car door.

2 and 3

Order No: PC08/1020/0017	Item	Damaged	Missing
Name: Mr ~~Bert Sandle~~ Burt Sandell	1 router antenna	bent	
Address: 14 Hayford Road	2 mouse		✓
Catford	3 computer screen	scratched	
London	4 keyboard	broken	
Postcode: SE10 ~~4QU~~ 4QY	5 power cable		no plug
Tel: 0208 411 4009	6 LH speaker	damaged	
Email: bsandell87@ ~~bdg.co.uk~~ pdq.com	7 RH speaker	hole in front	
	8 user manual		✓

4 Reporting damage
1 The box is damaged.
2 The overalls are torn.
3 There's a dent on one of the speakers.
4 There are some cracks on the radio.

Reporting something missing
1 The headphones are missing.
2 There are no pliers in the toolbox.
3 The power cable doesn't have a plug.
4 The radio has no antenna.
5 There's no user manual in the box.

3 Past events

1 1 Which year did you travel to the ISS?
2 When did you take off?
3 How did you travel into space?
4 What did you take with you?
5 What did you do on the ISS?
6 Did you repair the solar panel?
7 When did you leave the ISS?
8 When did you return to Earth?

2 1 I bought it 10 months ago.
2 I dropped it 4 weeks ago.
3 I brought it into the Service Department 10 days ago.
4 I sent my email 3 days ago.

4 Word list

1 bend / bent   lose / lost
break / broke   put / put
burn / burnt   sell / sold
buy / bought   send / sent
cut / cut   speak / spoke
drive / drove   steal / stole
fall / fell   take / took
fly / flew   tear / tore
go / went   write / wrote

2 1 insulation   4 hard hat   7 goggles
2 scaffolding   5 crane   8 overalls
3 sledgehammer   6 digger

REVIEW UNIT D

Section 1

1
1	long	7	length	13	width
2	wide	8	more than	14	length
3	depth	9	at	15	below
4	through	10	deep	16	through
5	More than	11	long		
6	depth	12	wide		

2
1 A: Hello. Can I help you?
   B: Yes. I'm building a wall and I need some cement.
   A: How much do you need?
   B: I need two bags, please. And I also need some sand.
   A: How many bags do you need?
   B: I need six bags, please.
2 A: Hello. What can I do for you?
   B: Do you have any paint?
   A: Yes. How much do you need?
   B: 10 litres, please. And I need some nails.
   A: How many packets?
   B: One packet, please.

Section 2

1

Verb	Past simple	Past participle
bend	bent	bent
build	built	built
burn	burnt	burnt
find	found	found
lose	lost	lost
pay	paid	paid
break	broke	broken
come	came	come
give	gave	given
go	went	gone

2
1 When did the digger drive into the shop window?
2 When did the thieves break into the office?
3 How much money did the mechanic find?
4 When did the builders take off the old roof?
5 Where did the scaffolding fall down?

3
A: Have you put up the scaffolding?
B: Yes, I have.
A: Good. Have you changed the power cable?
B: No, I haven't. I'll do it next week.
A: Have you bought the bricks?
B: No, I haven't. I'll do it next week.
A: Have you spoken to the supplier?
B: Yes, I have.
A: Good. Have you ordered the water tank?
B: No, I haven't. I'll do it next week.

9 Troubleshooting

1 Operation

1
1	supports	4	drives	7	propels
2	steers	5	pulls	8	release
3	controls	6	pushes		

2
1 What does the engine do?
   It drives the impeller.
2 What does the impeller do?
   It pulls water in and pushes it out.
3 What do the handlebars do?
   They steer the craft.
4 What do the levers do?
   They control the speed of the craft.
5 What does the seat do?
   It supports the rider.

3
1 The seat is mounted on the body.
2 The handlebars are mounted on the body.
3 The levers are attached to the handlebars.
4 The engine is mounted on the body.

2 Hotline

1
1	display	3	speaker	5	adapter
2	mouse	4	printer	6	power switch

2
1 The display is on.
2 The power switch is down.
3 The computer is connected.
4 The printer is on.

3 Dialogue 1: The computer was plugged in. The adapter wasn't connected to a power source.

Dialogue 2: The adapter was connected to a power source. The speaker wasn't connected to the adapter.

Dialogue 3: The display was working. The mouse battery wasn't charged.

4
1 No, it doesn't.
2 Is the power switch down?
   No, it isn't.
3 Are the loudspeakers connected to a power source?
   No, they aren't.
4 Is the adapter connected?
   Yes, it is.
5 Do the loudspeakers work?
   No, they don't.
6 Are the two LED lights on?
   Yes, they are.
7 Does the computer start?
   Yes, it does.
8 Do the loudspeakers work now?
   Yes, they do.

3 User guide

1 Open, Press, check, recharge, work, press, Close

2
1 If the LEDs aren't on, check the battery.
2 If the printer doesn't work, connect it to the adapter.
3 If the printer light isn't on, push the 'On' button.
4 If the batteries are old, replace them.
5 If the speakers don't work, connect them to a power source.
6 If it prints in black, press the button for 'Colour'.

3

1 Check	5 plug	9 unplug
2 plugged	6 Press	10 Press
3 Check	7 shuts	11 turns
4 connected	8 shut	

4 Word list

1 adapter, battery, computer, disk, disk drive, display, key, laptop, LED, modem, mouse, notebook computer, power button, power outlet, power source, router, screen, speaker, start button, switch

2
1 The rider releases the lever.
2 The fan pulls air in.
3 The rider can go backwards.
4 The engine is below the platform.
5 The fan stops and the airboard goes downwards.

10 Safety

1 Rules and warnings

1

1 safety helmet	3 safety boots
2 safety gloves	4 safety goggles

2
1 Don't smoke in the workshop.
2 Never use mobile phones in the workshop.
3 You must wear safety goggles when you use this machine.
4 You must never enter the cold store if you are alone in the factory.
5 Do not lift heavy weights by hand.
6 You mustn't use this machine without the guard.
7 Always read the manual before you service the machine.
8 Don't touch packets in the cold store without gloves.

3

1 drop / break	5 pick / burn
2 put / melt	6 touch / get
3 lift / hurt	7 use / trap
4 use / scratch	

2 Safety hazards

1
1 There is some liquid on the floor.
2 There is a hole in the outside door.
3 There is no fire exit.
4 There is a broken window.
5 There are some cables on a workbench.
6 There are no fire extinguishers in the factory.
7 There are two machine guards missing.
8 There are some damaged warning cones.

2
1 You could start a fire.
2 You might get an electric shock.
3 You could trip over them.
4 You might trap your hair in it.
5 You could fall into it.
6 You might injure your head.
7 You could burn your hand.

3
1 There were no fire extinguishers anywhere in the factory.
2 There was some food and drink on the workbenches.
3 There were some boxes of parts on the stairs.
4 The guard on one of the machines was broken.
5 There was some oil on the floor.
6 Two of the windows were broken.
7 The fire exit was locked with a padlock.
8 There was no key for the padlock.

3 Investigations

1

About the accident	Type of accident (tick)	About the injured person
Date: 29 March Time: 3.30 pm Location: No. 6 workshop	[✓] injured self [ ] injured somebody else [ ] slipped, tripped or fell [✓] lifted something [✓] dropped something	Name: Peter Graski Job title: Storeman Injury: Hurt his back and foot At work: No

2
1 First, where did the accident happen?
2 Was anybody hurt?
3 When did it take place?
4 What's the name of the injured person?
5 What does he do?
6 What's his job?
7 Did he injure anybody else?
8 What happened?

3

1 on	6 on	10 between
2 in	7 with	11 away
3 into	8 on	12 into
4 in	9 on	13 out
5 of		

4 Word list

1

1 dense cloud	5 circular saw
2 bare hand	6 electric shock
3 lighted match	7 high-voltage
4 near miss	

2

1 fire extinguisher	5 flight path
2 safety boot	6 mobile phone
3 safety hazard	7 building site
4 sea level	

3 altitude, aviation, distance, incident, investigation, runway, type, near miss

REVIEW UNIT E

Section 1

1
1	cushion	4	skirt	7	fibreglass
2	engines	5	platform	8	levers
3	fans	6	body	9	acceleration

2
1	can	5	is	9	have
2	doesn't	6	is	10	haven't
3	I've	7	have	11	does
4	there's	8	have	12	does

3 Turn the key to the right and press the starter button. If the engine starts, move the lever to 'D' and ride away. If the engine doesn't start, check the battery. If the battery works, check the starter motor. If the battery doesn't work, recharge the battery. If the battery still doesn't work, replace the battery.

Section 2

1
1 Turn off this machine after use.
2 Always use safety boots in the shipyard.
3 Drivers must report to the office.
4 Never ride on the forklift truck.
5 Do not use this machine without safety goggles.
6 You must not reverse without a supervisor.

2
1	inspected	7	was	13	hit
2	found	8	were	14	was
3	were	9	lifted	15	shouted
4	was	10	was	16	saw
5	didn't have	11	came	17	wasn't
6	were	12	moved		

3
1 Where did the incident happen?
2 When did it take place?
3 Did it take place on a ship?
4 What did the crane lift?
5 Was there a rope attached to the beam?
6 Did the beam hit the worker?
7 Was the worker hurt?

11 Cause and effect

1 Pistons and valves

1	tank	6	float
2	half-flush button	7	cable
3	full-flush button	8	flush valve
4	fill valve	9	tank
5	inlet pipe	10	rubber seal

2
allow it to do
cause it to do
let it do / make it do
prevent it (from) doing / stop it (from) doing

3
1 The pump causes the water to flow along the pipes.
2 The valves let air enter the tyres.
3 The valves prevent air (from) escaping from the tyres.
4 The sun makes the solar panel heat the water.
5 The cooling system stops the engine (from) getting very hot.
6 The closed inlet valve doesn't allow the water to flow out.

2 Switches and relays

1
1	switch	7	terminal
2	switch	8	catch
3	terminal	9	moving contact
4	electromagnet	10	fixed contact
5	moving contact	11	switch
6	fixed contact		

2 1c, 2a, 3b

3
1 F <u>Three</u> of the systems cause an alarm to sound.
2 T
3 F The ExitGuard works when somebody <u>breaks open the ExitGuard</u>.
4 T
5 F The burglar alarm works on the <u>doors and windows</u>.
6 T

3 Rotors and turbines

1
1	gear	4	blade	7	controller
2	brake	5	turbine	8	anemometer
3	housing	6	shaft	9	rotor

2
1	turbine	6	blades
2	anemometer	7	generator
3	controller	8	shaft
4	brake	9	housing
5	gear	10	rotor

3 1b, 2a, 3c, 4b, 5b

4 Word list

1
1	prevent	4	blow
2	expand	5	transmit
3	decrease	6	outlet

2
1	beep	5	dial tone
2	horn	6	siren
3	alarm bell	7	buzzer / door bell
4	click		

12 Checking and confirming

1 Data

1 speed, motors, antennas, instruments, tools, suspension, mast, robot, body, cameras, Mars

2
1	on	4	on	7	to	10	in
2	over	5	near	8	at	11	up to
3	at	6	around	9	from	12	at least

3
1 What is the underwater robot called?
2 How much does Jason weigh?
3 Where are the two robot arms?
4 How does it collect living things?
5 Where are the special tools?
6 How many dives has Jason 2 made?

2 Instructions

1 1d, 2a, 3e, 4b, 5c

6g, 7j, 8f, 9h, 10i

2 *Sample answers*

1 A car goes forwards and backwards.
2 A helicopter flies up and down.
3 A motorboat goes forwards and backwards.
4 A plane flies up and down.
5 A rover goes over rocks and holes.
6 A space rocket flies into space.
7 A truck goes forwards and backwards.

3
1 isn't moving
2 isn't coming
3 am bringing
4 is happening
5 Is the craft moving
6 am pulling
7 is happening
8 is coming
9 is sitting

3 Progress

1
1 Bring the large wrench from the workshop.
   Take the large wrench to the workshop. 10
2 Loosen the nuts on the supply pump.
   Tighten the nuts on the supply pump. 9
3 Remove the pump from the supply pipe.
   Attach the pump to the supply pipe. 8
4 Dismantle the water pump.
   Assemble the water pump. 7
5 Disconnect the valve from the pump.
   Connect the valve to the pump. 6

2
1 Yes. 17 May.
2 No. 17 May.
3 Yes.
4 No. 19 May.
5 Yes.
6 Yes.
7 No. 20 May.
8 No. 22 May.

3
1 They've removed the nose cone.
2 He hasn't taken a photo of the nose cone yet. He'll do it on 17 May.
3 They've inspected the fuel tank.
4 They haven't replaced the fuel pipe yet. They'll do it on 19 May.
5 He's attached the cables to the foot pedals.
6 He's installed the new valves.

4 Word list

1
1 dismantle
2 remove
3 replace
4 include
5 less than
6 under

2 laser beam, robot arm, six-wheel drive, science laboratory, suspension system, temperature range, waste tank

REVIEW UNIT F

Section 1

1
1 It makes the pressure inside the cylinder fall.
2 This allows a mixture of petrol and air to enter the cylinder.
3 This stops the fuel mixture (from) escaping.
4 This makes the pressure in the cylinder rise.
5 The spark plug lights the fuel and causes it to explode.
6 This lets the burnt fuel escape.

2
1 dam
2 gates
3 blades
4 turbine
5 shaft
6 generator
7 electricity
8 cables

Section 2

1
1 The rover is 2.2 metres high.
2 It has a length of 3 metres.
3 It has a weight of 1025 kilograms.
4 It has a six-wheel drive.
5 The wheels are made of aluminium and titanium.
6 The wheels are 52.5 centimetres in diameter.
7 It can move at a speed of up to 152 metres per hour.
8 It can operate in a temperature range from minus 40 degrees Celsius up to plus 40 degrees Celsius.

2
1 Have you analysed
2 analysed
3 Have you repaired it yet?
4 haven't
5 repair it
6 connected
7 We'll do that
8 you replaced it yet
9 did that on
10 Have you assembled it yet
11 assembled it on
12 replaced
13 doing
14 Have you serviced it yet
15 'll service it on